HELP!
My Dog is Destroying the Garden

How to have a garden friendly dog

Toni Shelbourne
&
Karen Bush

Other titles by the authors

The Truth about Wolves and Dogs
Toni Shelbourne *(Hubble & Hattie)*
Among the Wolves: Memoirs of a Wolf Handler
Toni Shelbourne *(Hubble & Hattie)*
Dog-friendly Gardening
Karen Bush *(Hubble & Hattie)*
The Dog Expert
Karen Bush *(Transworld)*
The Difficult Horse
Sarah Fisher and Karen Bush *(Crowood Press)*
HELP! My Dog is Scared of Fireworks
Toni Shelbourne and Karen Bush
HELP! My Dog Doesn't Travel Well in the Car
Toni Shelbourne and Karen Bush

Copyright © 2017 Toni Shelbourne and Karen Bush
Images copyright of:
Llama TTouch © Toni Shelbourne: Zebra TTouch © Sarah Fisher
Ear work A © David & Charles: Ear work B © Sarah Fisher
Bottle spinner © Maddy Casey: Real Dog Yoga © Toni Shelbourne
Confidence Course © Toni Shelbourne: Walking over course © Sarah Fisher
Escape proof fencing © ProtectaPet Ltd:
Stokenchurch Dog Rescue garden © Karen Bush
Walkway and pergola © Jacksons Fencing
Cover images © Toni Shelbourne, Karen Bush, Sue Purkiss

The right of Toni Shelbourne and Karen Bush to be identified as the authors of this work has been asserted in accordance with the Copyright Designs and Patents Act 1988.
All rights reserved. No part of this book may be reproduced or transmitted in any form without the prior written permission of the copyright holder.

ISBN: 1976563313
ISBN-13: 978-1976563317

DEDICATION
This book is dedicated to all our dogs,
who we have learned so much from,
and who continue to teach us.

ACKNOWLEDGMENTS
We should like to thank Sarah Fisher, Robyn Hood,
Ken Bush, Bob Atkins, Kate Hanley at f+wmedia,
David & Charles, Jo-Rosie Haffenden

For simplicity, throughout this book, dogs have been referred to as 'he'

Disclaimer
While the authors have made every attempt to offer accurate and reliable information to the best of their knowledge and belief, it is presented without any guarantee. The authors do not accept any responsibility in any manner whatsoever for any error or omission, or any loss, damage, injury, adverse outcome, or liability of any kind incurred as a result of the use of any of the information contained in this book, or reliance upon it. Please bear in mind that the advice in this book is not intended to replace veterinary attention. If in any doubt about any aspect of welfare, care and treatment, readers are advised to seek professional advice.

CONTENTS

Introduction	7
1 Why is it happening?	9
2 Keeping out of trouble	15
3 Training	21
4 Toilet time	33
5 Keep off!	37
6 Turf wars	47
7 Plants	55
8 Channelling behaviours	59
9 Fun & games	69
10 Taking it easy	81
Appendix 1 Dog Friendly Plants	111
Appendix 2 Poisonous plants	117
Appendix 3 Creating a sensory garden	119
Further Reading	123
Resources and Useful Contacts	125
About the Authors	131

INTRODUCTION

"My garden is being ruined!" – it is a cry we frequently hear, and the old myth that you can have a nice garden or you can have a dog, but you can't have both still continues to do the rounds. But it is just not true. If you need convincing, you'll find there are plenty of popular garden experts who have actively welcomed dogs into their lives and gardens, rather than shunning them as being too destructive. Amongst those who have shown that it is perfectly possible to combine dog ownership with beautiful gardens are Alan Titchmarsh (a history of Labradors), Carol Klein (a brace of Lakeland Terriers), Christine Walkden (Labrador), Charlie Dimmock (Newfoundland), Sarah Raven (mixed breed rescue), Alys Fowler (terrier), Bunny Guinness (assorted breeds including bull mastiffs, a Pyrenean sheepdog, a Rhodesian Ridgeback and currently a trio of terriers) and Monty Don, whose two Golden Retrievers currently regularly appear with him on BBC TV's *Gardeners World*. Chris Beardshaw even used his own dog to help inspire him when asked by Winalot to design a dog-friendly show garden at the prestigious Hampton Court Flower Show.

You don't however, need to be a green-fingered gardening guru to keep your garden looking good. The more high maintenance your garden, then obviously the more time and effort you will need to put into keeping your dog from spoiling it though, so if planning a makeover be realistic about what you can manage, and prepared to compromise. Both dogs and gardens can give so much pleasure but neither will thrive if there isn't some give and take along the way!

Of course it is inevitable that there will occasionally be accidents and sometimes a little damage, but you can minimise any adverse impact your dog might have: you certainly don't need to resign yourself to a trashed plot which resembles a prison exercise yard. By combining common sense with a little ingenuity it is perfectly feasible to achieve a harmonious fusion of lovely garden and idyllic dog-space. How you design and manage your garden is of course, ultimately entirely up to you, but you will find life much easier if you garden *with* your dog, rather than in spite of him! Think of it as a gardening challenge to rise to, rather than a gardening problem. Got a dog who likes to dig? Give him a place of his own where he can excavate to his heart's content. If he enjoys snoozing out there, then provide somewhere comfortable so he doesn't have to make his own nest right in the middle of your flower bed.

The only hard and fast rule when it comes to what you can include in your garden, is that the welfare of your dog always comes first. Gardens can, after all, be rebuilt and replanted, but your dog is irreplaceable - safety in the garden is paramount. Although this book does touch on some of the issues you should be aware of, it is mainly concerned with how to keep your garden from being wrecked. You can, however, find more comprehensive information on safety issues in Karen's book *Dog-friendly gardening* (see Further Reading for details)

Let's get started!

1
WHY IS IT HAPPENING?

It is pointless (and exasperating) repairing damage to your garden if it keeps recurring. The first thing you need to do therefore, is work out why it is happening, as this will help you to decide on the best course of action.

Who's to blame?
Firstly, make sure you have correctly identified the culprit; if you haven't actually seen your dog causing the damage, there is a possibility that he is quite blameless. It might be that the damage to your seed beds has been caused by neighbourhood cats toileting in the inviting finely cultivated soil; that those bald-looking areas in your lawn are not the result of dog pee but of leatherjackets; and the dug-up patches of turf are due to visiting wildlife. If you aren't sure, keep a close eye on him, or have him close by you at all times when outside: if the damage immediately stops, then maybe your dog is the culprit after all.

Interaction
Having ruled out bugs, wildlife and other neighbourhood visitors to your garden, make sure that you aren't unwittingly responsible for your dog causing damage.

You may need to rethink the way in which you interact with him outdoors - if you encourage rowdy games, then damage is invariably going to occur.

This doesn't mean you can't both have fun out there, simply that you should choose some different games to play; you'll find some suggestions in Chapters 9 and 10 for garden-friendly activities which can be just as satisfying as chasing after balls or playing tag or hide and seek. And unless you have a huge garden, they will be a lot safer in a small space too!

Environment

As well as your personal interaction with your dog, consider the way he interacts with the garden and its surrounding environs.

Making changes to the garden design, instigating some basic training, and maybe adding a feature or two specifically to engage him and provide an outlet for innate urges such as digging could be the solution; we'll take a look at these things in more detail in the following chapters.

Some things that may trigger behaviours damaging to your garden may be out of your control however, such as its location; for example, if it borders on footpaths with pedestrians and maybe other dogs passing by, your dog may become excitable or defensive. In addition to using screening to reduce outside stimuli, and in the short term employing distractions such as offering tasty treats, it may be necessary to do some specialised training with your dog on a one-to-one basis with an experienced trainer. Of course there may be as simple a fix as keeping him indoors at those times when things happen outside which disturb or excite him, such as hot air balloons passing overhead, or the local children walking past on their way to and from school.

Exercise

The garden shouldn't be viewed as somewhere you can turf your dog out to do his own thing as an alternative to taking him for a walk. Getting out and about is as important mentally for your dog as the physical exercise involved: and if you have a very active dog he'll probably need more space in which to run and let off steam than most gardens provide anyway.

Making sure your dog gets sufficient exercise away from home means that he will be less likely to trash your garden by racing around it, and it can instead become a place to relax in a calm atmosphere. If allowing free-running on walks is a problem due to behavioural issues or lack of recall at present, you can if necessary hire secure facilities. There is a Facebook page and website dedicated to helping owners find safe dog walking places (see Contacts and Resources); you might also try hiring the indoor school of a local equestrian centre or contacting nearby dog training clubs and boarding kennels who may be able to help out with facilities.

One other aspect which may be worth looking into if your dog has hyper tendencies, always on the go and seemingly inexhaustible no matter how much exercise he has, is his diet. Avoid foods which are full of artificial additives, and check that protein levels are appropriate to his level of activity. There is plenty of information available on the internet to help you in researching the best grub for your dog.

Boredom

It is worth thinking about your dog's lifestyle generally, as this can often be an underlying cause of garden damage. A bored dog is more likely to be destructive - although from his point of view he is simply creating his own entertainment. Making sure he gets enough exercise is essential, but is only a part of ensuring that he's a fulfilled and happy individual. Mental stimulation is just as important – dogs need to have their brains exercised as well as their bodies.

Providing 'brain games' for him can be a great way of engaging his grey matter, keeping him amused and sparing your garden from his unwanted attentions, and we have suggested a few of these in Chapter 9. You might also think of ways that you can incorporate some brain work into your daily walks, and maybe try a new activity such as Agility, Nose work, Obedience, Treibball and Rally-O: all things which are fun and require him to use both body and brain. If you have a working breed, even if you don't intend to round up sheep or take him shooting, there is no reason why you can't take him for herding or gundog training. By identifying and enabling him to satisfy his doggy nature, the more contented and amenable a companion he will be, as well as one less likely to unleash his own especial brand of creative garden design.

Growing up
Chewing is often due to boredom – but not always. Sometimes it is down to teething, or to simple curiosity, especially where puppies are concerned; they explore and learn more about the world with their mouths as well as ears, eyes, nose and paws. In addition to plants, your garden furniture, gates and fencing, tool handles, hosepipes, watering can spouts and all sorts of other objects may be subjected to your dog's teeth. Spray taste deterrents are worth a try but although they may work with some dogs, we know of many who aren't at all put off by them; they also need to be frequently

renewed to be effective. The best solution is to treat the problem in exactly the same way as you would in the house; teach him a 'leave it' command (Chapter 3) and provide things that he is allowed to exercise his jaws on. One of the handiest of these are Kongs which can be stuffed in advance and left ready to hand in the fridge or freezer for when needed. You'll find more information on these and how to stuff them in Chapter 10.

Stress
Chewing and digging can also be stress-related, and obviously, if this is the case, then the source of his anxiety will need to be identified and resolved; the signs aren't always easy to spot and can be overlooked or misinterpreted. For example, a dog that is constantly fooling around may genuinely be a bit of a clown – but odd though it may seem, such behaviour doesn't always necessarily denote a happy dog any more than a waggy tail does, and can also be an indicator of stress. The aid of an experienced and observant behaviourist can be useful in helping you to determine if stress is at the root of your dog's behaviour.

Digging can be a boredom-combatting ploy too, but it can also be an attempt to escape, to create a den, to reach something desirable in a neighbouring property, to cache food, or perhaps because you have moles or rats which he is going after. Some dogs do of course love to dig simply for the sheer pleasure of digging – but you can easily provide an outlet for this if it is in his genes by constructing a special digging pit for him (see Chapter 8)

2
KEEPING OUT OF TROUBLE

Most dogs enjoy being out in the garden, but it is wise to supervise him while he is out there! This will enable you to check he isn't getting up to mischief - and if you do spot him doing something you'd prefer he didn't, means that you can nip it in the bud straight away. Once you have taught him the 'garden rules' he is also more likely to stick to them if you are out there with him - if you are absent he might ignore them, in much the same way as many dogs will sneak onto an out-of-bounds sofa or bed for a nap while their owners are out.

There is another very good reason why you shouldn't leave your dog up to his own devices in the garden. Sadly, dog-napping is on the increase, with some pets being stolen to order, used in puppy farms, held for ransom or used as 'bait' by dog fighters. There have been many horrific stories about dogs being snatched from owners in the street, taken while tied up outside shops or left in cars, and more recently thefts have been occurring from gardens too, where you might have thought your dog would be safe. Even though you can see your dog from inside the house, he may be a tempting target for thieves if he appears to be out there on his own – and if they do go after him, you may not be best placed to do anything to prevent it or it may be unsafe for you to intervene.

There will be times however, when you are both

out in the garden but you need to concentrate on a task and can't keep your full attention on your dog. While some dogs may be content to simply lie near you and have a snooze – with a comfy bed or his blanket plus a chewy treat to encourage him to settle – others may take a keen and unwanted interest in what you are doing. A friend was putting out young plants one Spring; as she reached the end of the bed she realised that her dog had been quietly following along behind her and industriously 'helping' by uprooting each of the plants she had been so carefully planting ...

At those times when you can't pay much attention to what your dog is up to, or if you are making frequent trips in and out of the gate, you'll need to safely contain him. The easiest and simplest solution is to leave him indoors, and certainly if using machinery such as mowers, strimmers and clippers, this is the safest one. At other times there are alternatives which will allow him to enjoy being outside with you but will ensure he is not getting into trouble.

Playpen
A playpen can be perfect for puppies and small dogs – although make sure it is sturdy enough in construction and securely anchored so that the walls cannot be knocked down, and that the sides are high enough to prevent jumping or climbing over.

Crates
Another option is a crate: these come in all shapes and sizes including square, rectangular and tubular, and are made of a variety of materials including steel mesh, fabric and plastic. Whatever type of crate you select, the larger the better: as a minimum it must be

big enough to allow your dog to stand up, lie down and comfortably turn around.

If your dog is unused to being in a crate, you will need to first introduce it to him; do this indoors, as it will allow more frequent opportunities. Set up the crate with some comfy bedding inside, feed him his meals in there and pop toys and treats in for him to discover. This will encourage him to use it, and make it an inviting place with pleasant associations where he will voluntarily choose to spend time relaxing.

Never try and manhandle your dog inside, no matter how gentle you are about it. You can however, introduce a verbal cue 'Crate!' or similar whenever you spot him going into it, so that you can ask him to go in on those occasions when you want him to. Tossing a treat in there for him to eat will enable you to repeat and establish this process more quickly.

Leave the door open at all times so he can come and go as he wishes initially; only when he is happy to voluntarily spend time in there should you shut the door. This should be for just a minute or two at first; provide a long-lasting treat such as a tightly stuffed Kong, (see Chapter 10) or choose a time of day when he normally enjoys a nap so he is less likely to be concerned about it. Gradually you can increase the length of time you leave the door shut; how quickly you progress depends on how quickly he takes to the crate. Some dogs do enjoy 'denning' especially if the crate is covered, as it provides them with a private, quiet space where they can feel safe. Do not abuse this though, and never leave your dog crated for more than two hours, and never leave him unattended during the introductory process.

Once your dog is completely happy about being in the crate in your house you can begin to introduce it in the garden in much the same way, to ensure he is just as confident about being in it when it is in a different location. Although he may be happier to spend longer in it while indoors, don't leave him confined in it in the garden for more than an hour, and don't leave him in direct sunlight.

Location
As with a playpen, think carefully about where you site the crate in the garden – some dogs may become anxious if they cannot see you, so you will need to position it so he is able to keep you in sight. Avoid placing it in full sunlight as he will be unable to escape to a cooler spot. If necessary, provide shade with a garden parasol or similar: simply placing a sheet over the top may not be adequate, and can create a stuffy interior. On hot days or when conditions are very humid he may be happier and safer if left indoors.

Make sure he has access to water and check on him at regular intervals; and remember that as the sun moves, so will the patch of shade! If you go indoors, even if only briefly, let him out and take him with you, rather than make him an extra-easy target for thieves or vulnerable to teasing or even attack from passers-by. The same also applies if using a puppy pen, or a tether.

Tethering
Tethering is not the most ideal option: in very dry weather it can be difficult to get the stake into the ground, and if it has been wet it may be easily pulled out of the ground, especially by larger dogs. You also need to be able to keep half an eye on your dog in case he becomes entangled in the leash or chews through it. If you do decide you want to try this however, then an ordinary sturdy six foot leash is quite adequate; if it is longer it is more likely to lead to injury if he races after something and is then

pulled up hard when he reaches its fullest extent. Always use a quick release knot in case of emergencies.

Use a harness rather than a collar as this will help prevent neck injury (or accidental strangulation) should he suddenly rush forward, or jump up at you in greeting when you approach. As with a crate or playpen, avoid tethering him where he has no escape from full sunshine, ensure he has access to water, and provide a comfy bed or blanket to lie on plus a chewy treat to keep him occupied. Some dogs accept the restrictions of a tether with no fuss, but others may pull against it and will need to be taught not to fight it and to keep the leash slack. Clicker training can be helpful in tether-training him (see Further Reading and Contacts and Resources to find out more about clicker training), but it may be preferable to just use a different way of keeping him contained which he is happier about.

3
TRAINING

If you can teach your dog that it is fine to eat from his own bowl but not to help himself from your plate; that certain items of furniture or areas of the house are out of bounds; that toileting takes place outdoors, not inside, then there is no reason why you cannot apply the same training principles where your garden is concerned. It is not rocket science, merely a matter of setting up 'garden rules' in much the same way as you have 'house rules' for behaviours indoors. These should also include how you and the rest of the family interact with your dog outdoors – and everyone needs to be familiar with them and to stick to them. Dogs are much brighter than we often give them credit for, and provided everyone is consistent in their actions, most will pick up fairly quickly on what is and isn't allowed.

Positive interrupters
Initially of course, he will not know which things in the garden you'd prefer he didn't eat, chew or play with, so you will need to teach him. What trainers refer to as 'positive interrupters' can come in really handy in doing this. This is a great way of quickly getting your dog's attention, diverting him from doing something you feel is inappropriate but without making him feel that he is being scolded. It is very simple to teach – basically you say "Hey!" (or any other word that trips off the tongue easily)

and as soon as your dog looks at you, throw him a tasty treat. That is all he needs to do to earn a reward: simply to stop whatever he is doing for a moment to look at you. Practise this frequently, at first when there are few things to distract him. Every so often, say "Hey!" or whatever word you have chosen, and the instant he looks at you, toss the treat to him wherever he is. As he becomes quicker and more reliable in his response, you can ask him to hold your gaze for longer before rewarding him with a treat.

Having distracted his attention away from whatever undesirable activity he was engaged in (or about to do) you can then call him away and give him something he is allowed to have, such as a toy, a game with you, or a long-lasting chewy treat. In this way, he will learn that it is more rewarding to leave the object, or to cease the unwanted behaviour, than to ignore you and keep doing whatever it was. It can be a good idea to always wear a filled treat pouch when you are in the garden, so you are never caught out empty-handed!

There are times when you may need to be more specific about what you'd like your dog to do, and investing a little effort in some training will be time well-spent. It will benefit you in everyday life as well as making it easier to nip any unwanted behaviours in the bud, and to teach your dog the 'garden rules'. Even though you may be familiar with the following actions from basic training classes, it can be easy to let them lapse, and if this is the case it is well worth brushing up on them.

Leave it

This is a training essential; it can be helpful in all sorts of situations, such as stealing food, or scavenging when out on walks. In the garden it can be used to tell your dog to leave anything alone which he is showing too close an interest in – whether it be a plant, a newly dug bed, a recently topped up bird-table or a visiting hedgehog.

1.
Hold a fairly boring treat between finger and thumb. Offer it to your dog, with your palm uppermost, and allow him to take it, at the same time saying 'Take it!' in a bright tone. Repeat five or six times.

2.
Offer the food again, but without saying anything, and this time just as your dog moves to take the food, turn your hand over, closing it into a fist so that he cannot eat it. Don't stare at him, or speak to him; ignore him if he sniffs, nudges or paws at your hand – don't draw it back away from him, but keep it in the same place. The moment he moves his nose away from it, turn your hand over palm uppermost again, say 'Take it!' and reward him with the treat.

3.
Repeat this several times, varying between offering the treat, saying 'Take it!' and allowing him to have it, and turning your hand over and closing it into a fist to withhold it. Let him have more treats than you withhold.

4.
Most dogs quickly learn that as soon as you turn your hand over and make a fist they won't get the treat unless they move their nose away from it. Once this happens, attach a verbal cue to his action such as 'Leave!'

5.
When your dog is promptly offering the behaviour, try upping the stakes by offering a tastier treat.

6.
Vary the exercise by placing a treat on the ground

instead and covering it with your foot to prevent him getting it. At first he may try nudging, sniffing or pawing at it again. As before, the moment he moves his nose back away from it, reward him, but with a different treat given from your hand.

7.
Should you need to put this exercise into action in a real-life situation, praise and reward him lavishly. If you ignore him the moment he has left the object, he may not bother to pay attention to you the next time.

Give it

This is an important behaviour to teach your dog so that you can stay in control of games such as throwing balls or playing tuggy; it can be equally useful in the garden in case he decides to pick up anything he shouldn't. It is fairly simple to teach and you will be very glad you took the time to do so in the event of him scooping up anything potentially harmful.

1.
Have a brief tuggy game with your dog, using a toy he likes.

2.
When you want him to give up possession of the toy to you, draw it close to you with one hand, and keep it as still as possible, so the game is no longer as exciting.

3.
With your other hand, offer a really super-tasty treat, holding it close to his nose. In order to take the treat, he first has to let go of the toy. Make sure the treat is tempting enough – it helps if it is also strong smelling. If he prefers toys to food, offer to swap the one in his mouth for another higher-value toy instead.

4.
Have another brief game with the toy, and repeat the whole procedure as before.

5.
Keep practicing this several times a day over a period of several days. Once he starts to give up the toy quickly try bringing your free hand forward but without a treat in it and gently place it just under his chin. Anticipating a treat, he will release the toy – praise him and treat him immediately, and return to play. The hand below his chin will become the physical signal you use to ask him to give you whatever is in his mouth. At this stage you can also attach a verbal cue to the action, such as 'Give'.

6.
If your dog isn't food motivated or doesn't like to play tug but loves games of fetch, use two toys instead to teach the 'Give' command. Throw one toy, and as he brings it back, show him the other and indicate that you will throw it. As he drops the first toy in favour of chasing the second, say your verbal clue of 'Give'. He will soon learn it is worth dropping the toy in his mouth as it ensures the continuation of the game.

Come

A good recall can be as important in the garden as when out on a walk. It is, however, something that many owners struggle with – the secret is to make it fun and really rewarding: rewards have to be highly desirable, and you need to be the most exciting person in the world to be with at that moment. Experiment with finding which treats he likes the best – it may be a piece of smelly sausage for some or cheese for others. Whenever you call him to you, and after you have given him a food treat, have a quick but really exciting game and make a big fuss of him, so that coming to you has really good associations and he will be happy to leave other temptations. Don't use your recall for things he finds unpleasant, such as having his nails clipped or to give him a dose of medicine. You can even make a game out of doing recalls – for example, you'll find details in Chapter 9 of how to play the Boomerang Game.

1.
Begin teaching a recall indoors, as it will be the least distracting environment. Walk a few feet away from your dog, show him that you have a treat, call his name and say 'Come' or 'Here'. Make your tone of voice a light, happy one with an upwards inflection, as this will be more encouraging.

2.
When he comes to you, give lots of praise and reward him. Feed him tiny pieces of that super-tasty treat for thirty seconds; this might seem like overdoing it, but you want your dog to feel that coming to you has really been worth it. It is also a good way of encouraging him to hang around you rather than grabbing a single treat and running off again.

3.
Practise this as many times a day as you can, and as he becomes really quick to respond, start to practise in a variety of places around the house, and then move outdoors to the garden.

4.
Until coming to you when you call him is an instant and virtually automatic response, call your dog only when you are certain that he will respond, so that he doesn't learn that ignoring you is an option. If he is intent on something else, wait until he has lost interest in it before you call him; if it is important for him to leave the object and you haven't yet

established a 'Leave' command either, then walk over, quietly and calmly clip a leash on him and lead him away from it. Do be aware of your personal safety, and if you have a dog who resource guards high value items, then use those extra yummy treats to lure him away before clipping on the lead.

5.
Always praise and reward your dog when he does come to you, even after you have finished training the behaviour and have a reliable recall. If it stops being a rewarding thing to do, he will stop doing it!

Off!

If you already have an 'off' command which you use in the house when your dog clambers onto the sofa, then you can just as easily apply it to the flower beds in the garden too. If not, then it is fairly simple to teach, but you need to be really consistent. If you are out in the garden with him and allow him to trample around on the flower beds on some occasions but not at other times, it will be confusing for him.

Be prepared and carry a treat bag filled with plenty of yummy treats, or have your dog's favourite toy in your pocket each time you go out together in the garden.

Bear in mind that this is one of those behaviours that may not stick if you are not actually around. Even after he has learnt that flower beds – like sofas and human beds in the house – are out of bounds to him, he may still be inclined to trespass on them when you aren't present!

One other point is that if you have taught your dog not to jump up at you using the word 'Off', then you should pick a different cue word, such as 'Out', so as to avoid any confusion.

1.
If you see your dog on, or about to step on, a flower bed, quickly get a treat ready in your hand and call his name or use your positive interrupter word. Having gained his attention, let him see you throw the treat onto the grass. As he moves onto the lawn say the command word you have chosen.
2.
Do this *every* time you spot him on flower beds. The throwing of the treat will also eventually become a visual cue for him, which dogs seem to understand more easily.

On leash
You may find a six foot long (2m) trailing leash attached to a harness useful during garden training. Keep an eye on your dog at all times while he is wearing it in case he becomes tangled up in it or chews at it. It can be handy as a way of gently containing or removing your dog from places you don't want him to be (such as stepping onto flower beds) without physically manhandling him until you have an effective "off" command. Don't grab, tug, jerk, or pull on it, but be tactful: firm if necessary, but never forceful. You may find it helpful to read Robyn Hood's book on leash-walking to help you use it appropriately and effectively (see Further Reading)

Wait
A 'wait' command can be invaluable in many situations; for calming a dog who rushes out into the garden barking and charging around for example, stopping him running onto flower beds, or charging back into the house with muddy paws. It can even be a life saver on occasion – such as keeping him from racing out of the front door or

through the garden gate if someone has left it open.

1.
Start off with your dog on the leash and standing in front of you so that you are facing each other.

2.
Ask him to wait, using a verbal command and hand signal (hand up, showing the palm); pause for a second and then reward him with praise and a treat. Gradually begin to increase the duration, a second at a time, before rewarding him, until he remains stationary for up to 30 seconds.

3.
Now ask him to wait as before, but take a step backward away from him and then step back again to your original position. Praise and reward him.

4.
Build this up gradually, by taking a step backward, and counting to five before stepping back to your original position in front of him. Slowly increase the number of steps you take to two, three and more, and begin to increase the length of time as well as the distance that you are from him.

5.
If he tries to follow you, quietly return him back to his place and next time move a little more slowly, or less far away from him, or for a shorter time.

6.
Vary the exercise by taking steps sideways as well as increasing distance and duration. Eventually you should be able to walk all the way around him without him moving. Practise in lots of different places, such as at doors, gates, when getting in and out of the car, and once he shows reliability, try it off leash.

In!
If your dog has a tendency to bark in the garden at

passing people, birds flying overhead, or maybe a neighbour's dog or cat, an "in" command can be handy.

1.
Start teaching this standing directly outside the back door, and at a time when there are no distractions. Gain your dog's attention and let him see that you have a tasty treat or a favourite toy. Throw it in through the open door, and as he goes in to retrieve it, say "in!"

2.
Most dogs find this fun as well as rewarding, and do not take long to cotton on to what you want. Eventually, your hand movement will become a visual cue, together with the verbal one, to go indoors.

3.
As your dog gets the idea, begin slowly moving further away from the door – short distances at first and gradually increasing them. Don't forget to always reward him!

Teach a pee cue
Teaching your dog a 'pee command' is simple to train and can be really useful. It can help him to know what you expect of him, when and where. Once learned, it will mean you will no longer have to stand in the rain or cold for ages waiting for him to empty his bladder last thing at night, or if you take him away on holiday and he is not sure if or where he is allowed to go.

It also enables you to ensure he has relieved himself before setting out on car journeys, or visiting other people's gardens. Just as importantly for your garden, it makes it easier for you to teach him to pee in a single designated place in your garden, rather than spreading it around!

1.
Think of a word that you want to use as your pee cue. The most common words or phrases used are 'busy, busy' or 'hurry up', but you can choose whatever you like, as long as it is something you don't use often during everyday life, and which won't be embarrassing for you, or offensive to others, to use in public.

2.
Whenever you take your dog out on a walk, or into the garden to toilet, wait until you see him actually peeing; only once he is in full flow say your chosen pee cue eg 'Busy, busy' or 'hurry up' and keep repeating it until he is done.

3.
Once he has finished give him a huge amount of praise and a yummy treat (make sure you have remembered to take the treat out with you!) It is important that you give him the treat there and then so he makes the connection between the action and reward.

4.
Repeat this stage for a few days; you will find that you soon learn to recognise the visual cues he gives, just before he starts to toilet. Now is the time to introduce your pee cue, just before, or right as, he starts to go. Be sure that he is definitely about to start before you use the verbal cue though, or he won't get it. Do keep rewarding and heaping on the praise as he finishes.

5.
After a few more days, try giving the command when he looks as though he might be interested in going; give the pee cue and repeat it as he goes, praising lavishly and rewarding with a treat as he finishes, just as you have done previously. If you have misjudged matters, don't worry; simply repeat the earlier steps

to establish more firmly the connection between the pee cue and action and to give you more time to learn the little giveaway signs that he wants, or is about, to spend a penny.

6.

Eventually, you will be able to say the word and it will encourage him to toilet; do continue to reward, with praise and/or a treat, even after he knows the command, to reinforce the behaviour. Some dogs are very quick to pick this cue up, while others can take a little longer to catch on; but all dogs can be taught it, regardless of age.

4
TOILET TIME

One of the major causes of damage to your garden is likely to be your dog's urine, due to its high nitrogen content. While nitrogen can be a marvellous fertiliser when used in the right proportion, in excessive quantities it will result in 'burning' of plants instead – which explains why those dead brown patches on the lawn are often surrounded by long, lush growth round the edges, where the nitrogen is less concentrated.

You will sometimes hear it said that the urine of female dogs is more damaging than that of males, but the pee of both is the same. It is their toileting habits which differ, and which is probably responsible for the idea. Although some girls will urine mark like the boys, the majority tend to squat and will empty their bladders completely in one go on the ground, resulting in a hefty dose of grass-killing nitrogen on one spot.

Male dogs on the other hand – once they've learned to cock a leg – are more likely to deliver urine against vertical surfaces as well as to spread it around, treating it as a scent-marking exercise as much as a bladder-emptying opportunity. It is the quantity rather than the quality of pee which does the damage, but repeat visits can be cumulative and just as detrimental, although the effects of boy-peeing is more likely to be noticed in your flower borders and lawn edges.

There are several ways you can tackle the problem, which are all simple and cheap:

- **Go out**

The first of these solutions is obvious and common-sense: as well as taking your dog out for walks where he can enjoy free-running, play and socialising opportunities, take him out for additional briefer outings on the leash as well, so that he has plenty of opportunities to spend a penny.

- **Dilute it**

If you do spot your dog having a pee in the garden, as soon as he has finished, dilute it straightaway by watering the spot with three or four times the volume of water. Leave a filled watering can in readiness at all times, and train the rest of your family to use it if you aren't around yourself to apply garden first aid!

- **Anti-burn products**

You can buy a variety of commercial products which, when added to your dog's water or food, profess to prevent 'lawn burn'. Some of these are harmless, but we would suggest that you avoid giving your dog anything which states that it changes the pH of the urine. This applies both to commercial products and those frequently-recommended DIY fixes that aim to do the same thing, including feeding tomato juice, vinegar or baking soda. This could potentially lead to health issues such as bladder infections, crystals, and bladder stones – and is likely to have little benefit for your lawn anyway, as it is the high nitrogen content, not the acidity of the pee which is damaging. In a healthy dog, the urine pH is between 5.5 – 7 and as most grasses will tolerate a pH within the ranges of 5.6 - 6.8 or slightly higher, this isn't really an issue to worry about.

- **Deal with other culprits**

Before simply writing them off as being due to your dog's toileting habits, check any dead patches of lawn more closely as they may be due to other causes, ranging from grubs to scalping with the mower. Bear in mind too, that if your garden receives regular visits from foxes, their urine will be every bit as damaging as that of your dog, and you may need to give some thought to ways of discouraging them.

- **Create a 'pee place'**

Creating a dedicated toilet area can save the rest of your garden from a lot of pee-inflicted damage. Don't expect grass – or anything much else – to thrive in the immediate area though, so if not properly planned it can end up looking like an eyesore and smelling a whole lot worse.

If you want to encourage your dog to use it, the surface of the area should be absorbent enough that he won't get splashed, and comfortable underfoot. It also needs to be washable, which rules out bark chips, sand and other similar surfaces. This is where artificial grass (see Chapter 6) can really come into its own, as it looks attractive, won't die back or become unpleasantly slippery underfoot, and is easy to disinfect and wash off on a regular basis.

Male dogs will appreciate a vertical surface to pee against, and you can buy pheromone impregnated 'pee posts' especially for this purpose. If you would prefer something which is a little more attractive, you can make a feature out of a necessity by placing a piece of statuary out there instead, or maybe a column with a sundial or bird bath set on the top – above pee-level, obviously – or a bird table perhaps.

If your boy dog is a little slow to cotton on to the idea, simply collect a bit of his pee and anoint it for him.

Encourage your dog to use the toilet area you have created by taking him to it on the leash each time he goes out in the garden. Wait until he has had a pee, praise and reward him and only then take off the leash and allow him to have a game and some fun.

Some dogs learn very quickly to use their special pee place; after a week of taking him there try letting him loose to see if he has got the idea. If not, carry on taking him there until the penny drops, so to speak.

Teaching your dog to use the pee place will be made even easier if you teach a pee cue – you can find more about this in Chapter 3.

- **Poo**

Unlike pee, dog poo is not actually harmful to your garden, but scattered deposits don't look nice, quickly start to smell in warm weather and will attract those garden arch-enemies, slugs and snails. It is equally unpleasant when you or your dog invariably accidentally treads on a pile of poo; and of course it can contain all sorts of nasty bacteria and leaving it hanging around increases the risk of reinfestation from worm eggs.

As with peeing, you can teach your dog to use a dedicated toilet area, in the same way. Pick up any poo as soon as you see your dog going, and dispose of it: there are many different ways of doing this, but one novel idea you might like to consider is investing in a dog poo wormery. The compost created could allow your dog to actively contribute to the wellbeing of the garden!

5
KEEP OFF!

Just as your dog soon learns which areas in the house are out of bounds, so you can teach him that there are places in the garden you'd prefer he kept his paws and nose out of.

You'll find some suggestions about how to teach 'off' commands in Chapter 3, but may also find it helpful to consider additional ways to encourage him to leave your flower beds alone.

Avoid adding temptations

The allure of commonly-used fertilisers such as blood, bone, feather and fishmeal, and manures (both fresh and in the form of dried pelleted chicken manure) may be too difficult for even the best-trained dog to resist.

Digging them in well won't help much as the scent will still linger and he may dig in those areas trying to locate the source.

If he starts ingesting the soil – or worse still, should he actually get hold of a packet – it isn't going to do him much good either, and could potentially lead to problems such as pancreatitis and blockages.

Do a little research and look into other organic sources of nourishment for your plants, such as using grass clippings, applications of liquid seaweed, and making your own comfrey and nettle fertilisers which will have minimal appeal.

Plant densely
Planting as densely as possible is a brilliant way of ensuring that as little soil as possible is exposed to tempt your dog into digging in flower beds, or lounging around on them when they have become nicely sun-warmed. Do not however, plant prickly shrubs and plants; it is not necessarily a deterrent to all dogs, especially if in a state of excitement, and could cause injuries to skin and eyes.

Define the edges
Your dog may not perceive much difference between where the lawn ends and the flower beds start. When teaching him to stay off the beds, it can therefore be helpful if you can create some obvious contrast between them. Edging can be helpful in defining edges and comes in all sorts of options and materials; if this is not to your taste, you can use a change in texture to create a very obvious distinction instead, such as gravel mulches, or shells. Another way in which you can create an invisible line is to use scent – dogs have a much keener sense of smell than we do, so it doesn't need to be anything really overpowering. Use something which has a distinctive odour, is non-toxic and cheap and easy to replace as required – orange or lemon peel can work well. There is also a plant nicknamed the 'Go-away Plant'; *Plectranthus ornatus,* also sold under the names of 'Scaredy Cat' or *Coleus canina,* is supposed to have a sufficiently unattractive smell to dogs and cats that they will avoid it.

Make it uncomfortable
Gravel, stone chippings and cobbles are available in all sorts of colours and when used as a mulch on beds can look fabulous. It can also help in weed

suppression and moisture retention – but more importantly from your point of view will create a surface which is uncomfortable underfoot for your dog to walk or lie on and will discourage him from digging. The obvious change in textures will also make it easier for him to discern the difference between the bed and the lawn when training him to keep off.

Digging

When you are engaged in digging over beds, your dog may well be fascinated by the newly-turned soil – or perhaps read it as being a permissible activity for him too! If you need to do a spot of digging, then keep an extra vigilant eye on him until you are sure that he has lost interest in the area. This could of course, be the perfect opportunity to create a 'no-dig' garden instead, which will enable you to spend more quality time out there with your dog, as well as not putting any ideas into his head.

A membrane can work well as a way of suppressing weeds in beds should you opt for a 'no-dig' strategy, but should your dog decide to do a little excavating, a quite extraordinary amount of devastation can be caused if it is discovered and dragged out. Don't lay a membrane therefore, until you have some training in place – or if it is already in position prior to getting your dog, then make training an 'off' command and if necessary creating a special digging zone for him a gardening priority.

Some dogs really love to dig, and need no encouragement to get their paws dirty – and not just the terrier breeds traditionally associated with such activities. If digging is in his blood, then no matter how much training you do with him, you'll find it difficult to keep him from it – and not just in flower beds either. Succeed in stopping him from excavating in one spot and he'll probably just move on to a different place, so rather than trying to thwart his natural instincts (and doing something which gives him pleasure) you may be more successful and have a happier dog if you simply channel the behaviour instead, by giving him a special digging place of his own. You will find more information on this in Chapter 8.

On the other hand, if your dog is digging specifically with escape in mind or to reach something outside the garden, rather than for the sheer pleasure he derives from it, then a digging pit is probably not going to be the right solution for you. Such tunnelling efforts usually take place alongside a perimeter fence; placing a drift of large cobbles may be enough to deter him and can look attractive, but if he is really determined you may need to create a more solid barrier. Digging a trench alongside the fenceline and burying chicken wire or steel mesh is often advocated, but is not ideal as dogs can seriously injure paws and mouths digging and biting at it. Better to line the trench with bricks, breeze blocks or cement before covering it again with soil and/or turf – but although an effective barrier it may not prevent your dog from continuing to dig, working his way along the fenceline. More effective, and also the simplest option is to lay paving slabs along the length as described below in *Rethink your borders,* and this will also prevent most wildlife from tunnelling into your plot from outside.

As well as taking preventive measures, turn detective and try to determine the cause as additional action may be needed; failure to remedy the underlying cause can lead to a very unhappy dog who may develop other challenging behaviours. Is there a dog or other animal in a neighbouring property that he is trying to reach? Or if he/she is entire, there may be an irresistibly strong urge to get out, and neutering might be the solution. Perhaps something in the garden or nearby in the environment is worrying him and causing him to seek escape. If necessary, consult an experienced behaviourist who may be able to cast a fresh eye on the matter.

Location, location, location ...
It is of course obvious, but often overlooked – before creating a new bed in the garden, think carefully about the best place to put it, not just for the most aesthetically pleasing effect, but to minimise damage from your dog. If you put it slap bang in the middle of the route he always takes to visit his toilet place at the end of the garden for example, the chances are that he will continue to use that same direct route, regardless of the fact there is now a flower bed in the way.

Rethink your borders
Flower beds are most often set around the edges of the garden and in most cases this is actually the best place for them if you have a dog. Unless, that is, you have a dog who likes to patrol the perimeter of his territory; especially if your garden is adjacent to others, or to footpaths which get regular foot traffic passing by, then they may be liable to end up getting trashed. If your dog can see through your current fencing, then changing it to panel or lap fencing, or erecting some kind of screening will create more privacy, obscuring his view of the outside world and minimising disturbances.

You can't do much about the sounds he may still hear though, (although acoustic fencing may help reduce it) and if they cause him to continue to force his way through even the densest of planting to try and find out what is going on, then a different tactic will be needed. In such instances, it can be easiest to go with the flow rather than fighting it, making a design feature out of a necessity by creating a perimeter path with beds set inside it, so that your dog has easy access to the edges of the garden.

Paved walkway with pergola *(photo: Jacksons Fencing)*

With a little imagination, this can become a really attractive feature: creative use of paving can be a good start, and will also prevent any tunnelling under fences. Adding trellis and a pergola system will produce an elegant cloister style arcade which will increase your vertical planting area and become an inviting walkway for humans to stroll around too.

Try an alternative
Raised beds
Raised beds can be another way of keeping your

dog from trashing them – although this does of course depend on their height and the athleticism of your pet: some training may still be required to discourage him from viewing them as being an interesting addition to his playground. It will however, reduce the amount of 'watering' your plants receive from male dogs!

There will be other benefits too, as the soil will warm up more quickly, stay warm for longer, they'll create added interest through height, and there will be less strain on your back as you tend your plants.

Do however, bear in mind that escape artists may use it as a handy leg-up over garden fences; in such instances fencing may need to be made escape-proof by adding an inward-angled top line *(left)*.

(photo: ProtectaPet)

Containers

If raised beds aren't feasible, there is always the option of container planting instead. As with raised beds, it will be more difficult (although not impossible) for him to dig up or pee on your plants, he won't run through them – and provided you keep your pots filled with foliage or flowers, he won't be tempted into using them as a garden lounger.

Collections of containers can look fabulous in their own right, particularly if your garden is flat and lacking in focal points. By using a variety of sizes and heights of containers, and setting some on bricks or old car tyres, you can create graduated levels to produce a looser, more informal arrangement than with raised beds. You can also, of course, move them around as the fancy takes you, so that the form is less fixed, and should you move house, will be able to take your plants with you.

Because container growing also enables you to create perfect soil conditions, and to place them in the most auspicious position, it also allows you to grow plants that might not otherwise thrive in your garden soil. They will need regular watering in dry weather but otherwise you may find them easier to tend than flower beds as well as being a way of keeping your dog from damaging the contents.

You can buy containers or make your own by upcycling items which might otherwise be discarded: crates and packing cases, cleaned drums, old sinks, leaking buckets, watering cans and old builder's woven nylon rubble bags – anything that holds soil and can have drainage holes added.

Old car tyres can also be pressed into service, and if you look online, you will discover any number of ingenious ways in which they can be used.

When selecting containers, preferably choose those which are either the same width or wider at the base than at the top, as they will be more stable and less likely to be blown over by winds or accidentally knocked over by boisterous behaviour from your dog.

Go vertical
Especially if space is at a premium, using vertical space may be the answer – not all flower beds need be at ground level! There are many ways in which you can create vertical beds which will be out of your dog's way; as well as traditional window boxes

and hanging baskets, you can create wall planters made from wooden pallets, buy or make hanging containers with pockets to add plants, or maybe try your hand at kokedama (Japanese Moss Balls) which can look stunning.

Compost Bins

It is not just flower beds which you want to discourage your dog from jumping around on or digging in, but also the stuff that will eventually be nourishing them – the contents of your compost bin. This is not just because of the mess he can make, but because of the potential for harm if he gobbles up any toxic fruit and veggie scraps or inhales moulds: slow worms and snakes such as adders and grass snakes are also often attracted to them by their warmth as they decompose. If you cannot reliably fence it off so he cannot access it, then use an enclosed system such as the 'Dalek' style plastic bins – but don't penny-pinch: buy one which is sturdily made with a lid that cannot be easily flipped off.

6
TURF WARS

A nice grassy lawn looks great, and provides the perfect surface for your dog to play games or simply lounge around on. It is also eco-friendly, helping to reduce carbon dioxide emissions, and on a hot summer day can have a significant cooling effect – a lawn can be as much as 9 to 12°F (5 to 7 °C) cooler than bare soil, concrete or asphalt.

On the downside, your lawn is also likely to be the area most susceptible to damage if you have a dog - although to be fair, it isn't always him who is to blame. Before pointing a finger at him, check whether there are other culprits either responsible or at least contributing to it, such as leatherjackets and chafer grubs.

Bald or dead areas of lawn may also be due to soil damage, lack of water, spilt petrol from the mower when refilling the tank, the presence of tree roots, scalping of higher spots in uneven lawns, or possibly a variety of lawn diseases. Visiting wildlife such as badgers and foxes may also scrape at the surface or dig holes in search of food or as part of toileting activities.

Keeping your lawn in shape

If you want to keep your lawn looking good and in the best possible shape to withstand your dog, it helps if you follow a few basic ground rules:

- Don't play games which involve zooming around – save them for when out on walks. At home encourage different quieter, less damaging games and activities; you'll find some suggestions in Chapter 9.
- As much as possible, try to avoid walking on snow-covered grass, as this can damage the turf beneath. Frozen grass will also suffer from too much activity on it.
- Don't allow the grass to grow long and then cut it back drastically, as this stresses it: if in doubt the general rule of thumb is to never remove more than one third of the length in a single cut. Regular mowing helps keep the grass healthy (and makes it easier for you to spot and pick up any poo) but don't scalp it, as this makes it vulnerable to burning by the sun in hot weather. The experts recommend an ideal length of around 1-1.5 inches (2.5–4cm) long. Make sure the mower blades are sharp, and never mow when the grass is wet or frosty.
- Check out the tips in Chapter 4 about toileting, as doggy pee can be a major cause of patchy lawns.
- Dogs (and quite often humans as well) are likely to take the most direct routes across the garden rather than sticking to winding paths. Consequently, those areas that get a lot of foot traffic – for example a regular route taken to a toileting area – may suffer from soil compaction. Use a garden fork (or buy a purpose made tool to do the job) and use it to aerate the area and help with drainage. Alternatively, lay a pathway.
- If you have fence-to-fence lawn and find that damage occurs to the edges, rather than the

central portion, due to your dog patrolling the perimeter of his territory, it may be easier to go with the flow and make a feature of it instead by creating a walkway (see Chapter 5).

Repairing damage

Mild lawn burn caused by urine will often repair itself, given a little time and provided you can discourage your dog from continuing to repeatedly pee in the same place. Give it a helping hand by using a garden fork to create lots of holes and water liberally to dilute the excess nitrogen. More severely damaged spots can be repaired by cutting out the burnt area and either replacing with new turf or levelling and reseeding. Both these options are only going to be worth taking the effort over if you are able to keep your dog off while the new grass establishes itself, and are prepared to teach him to use an alternative dedicated toileting area, otherwise he will return to his habitual spots.

New lawn

If the lawn has been damaged so extensively that it is beyond repair, you may need to think about replacing it in its entirety. This is a pretty major decision since apart from the expense involved, there is also the inconvenience. If you reseed (the cheaper option) you won't be able to use the area for some time, and even if you returf, although you will have an instant lawn, you will still need to give it time to settle in and establish itself.

Choose the right sort of grasses – ones which are appropriate for your soil and climate, and that are fairly robust. Hardwearing mixes containing fescues and ryegrasses may not produce a luxury lawn look, but will be better able to withstand wear and tear. A chat with your seed or turf supplier will help you to decide on what will best suit your requirements.

Most importantly of all, bear in mind that unless you change the way in which the lawn is used or remedy whatever wrecked it the last time, a new one will quickly go the same way as the old one and be a waste of time and money. It might be worth considering whether a different surface might work better – see *Faking it* below.

Faking it

The smaller your garden is, the more your lawn will suffer from wear and tear. If you have a single, small, well behaved and calm dog, this may be fairly minimal and easily repairable; but where you have larger, multiple or highly active dogs you can find yourself fighting a losing battle. There will always be those dogs, who no matter how much alternative entertainment you provide, or how many walks you take them on will still joyously race round the garden – for some it is just too hardwired. In wet weather they can rapidly convert a grassy lawn into a muddy bog whilst in summer it becomes an arid dust bowl.

The solution may be to simply stop fighting a losing battle and do away with the grass altogether: for example, a friend has opted for creating a novel beach-style garden using sand, which her dogs love, and requires only an occasional raking to keep it tidy. The most commonly considered alternatives to lawn however, are more usually paving, decking, gravel or bark chippings – or combinations of one or more of these. Where your dog is concerned, these can have both plus and minus points:

Paving can look attractive with plenty of choice of shapes, colours and textures. You can also add interest by mixing with contrasting frost proof bricks, clay pavers, cobbles, timber and railway sleepers. Small 'planting pockets' can be created by leaving gaps between paving slabs for plants which don't mind occasionally being trodden on, such as thyme (*Thymus pseudolanuginosus* or *Thymus serpyllum*). It is easy to clean; but on the minus side can be an unforgiving surface for playing even gentle games on, and unless cleaned once or twice a year with a power washer to remove build ups of algae can become discoloured, and treacherously slippery in wet weather. It is also not great for the environment and rain drainage: it has become such a serious issue in fact, that regulations have been introduced by the government which may require you to apply for planning permission before paving over your garden.

Pressure treated hardwood decking can be an attractive, long lasting and easily cleaned feature which is available in a range of styles and stains. If there are gaps underneath it can however, become a refuge for rats, and as with paving slabs, does not provide an ideal surface for playing games on, will require an annual clean to remove grease and discoloration plus occasional brushing, and can be slippery when wet.

Gravel is a relatively cheap and freer-draining alternative to paving and can provide a low maintenance surface: all weeds and grass will need to be removed, the surface levelled and a weed proof membrane laid before putting down the gravel, which will need to be around 1 inch (2.5cm) deep. As with paving slabs, you can create planting pockets by cutting holes in the membrane to grow plants through. The disadvantages are that it can be difficult to pick up poop without collecting a bit of gravel at the same time, and many dogs really dislike walking on it, will be reluctant to lounge on it, and it is not a surface conducive to playing games on.

Bark or ***wood chippings*** are also fairly cheap to buy, easy to lay, and provide a free draining surface which is comfortable underfoot. As with gravel, it needs to be laid over a weed proof membrane, although in time as the surface breaks down they will start to grow in the bark layer. You may need to create an edge to minimize migration to other areas of the garden, and as it degrades it will need topping up. It can look very dark and oppressive, may feel a bit slimy when wet, and go mouldy; it is as difficult to pick poop up from as gravel – and neighbourhood cats and urban foxes also often home in on it as a great toileting area. Where it has been toiled on, it tends to hold the smell and is hard to maintain a degree of hygiene, which can be an important consideration if you have small children.

Playground rubber matting is a less conventional choice: it is available in a variety of colours, and virtually maintenance free, but although practical and durable, can look rather severely functional. If you don't mind adopting a synthetic alternative, but would prefer something a little easier on the eye and more in keeping with the appearance of a traditional garden, there is always the option of artificial grass.

Artificial grass has come a long way in recent years and these days can look incredibly realistic. Soft underfoot and low maintenance, it is becoming increasingly popular as a way of achieving the look of a lawn in difficult areas where grass doesn't thrive. It has acquired a somewhat controversial reputation, but the majority of the negative comments seem most often to be voiced by those who have no first-hand experience of it. Obviously, if you can manage to grow grass it is worth putting the time and effort into it, as it is the best and most ideal surface; but in smaller gardens, especially if they are also shady, a natural lawn simply may not cope no matter how much tender loving care it receives.

In its favour, everyone, human and canine, will benefit from the surface all year round: properly laid it will withstand a lot of activity, and it will be possible to run around out there in all weathers without slipping or churning up the grass, and there will be no more mud tracked into the house. Interestingly, dogs do not seem to feel the same urge to dig in it – although this is not necessarily a guarantee of good behaviour! It needs no mowing, weeding or fertilising, just occasional brushing and washing with a hosepipe. It is easy to pick up any poop, and it can be disinfected, which is a real plus if you have young children sharing the area. Admittedly, because it does not respire like real grass, on sunny days it is warm rather than cool to lie on, but most dogs seem to enjoy this.

The biggest criticisms of artificial grass are that because it is manufactured it carries its own carbon footprint, that it doesn't photosynthesise and doesn't offer a habitat for insects and wildlife. However, a well-manicured mown lawn offers only a very limited wildlife habitat; and if it has deteriorated into a bald patch of hard-baked earth in summer which turns into a muddy bog in winter, then even less will be in evidence. The lack of eco-friendliness can be compensated for by creating beds and filling containers with wildlife-friendly planting, adding climbers and hedging around the edges, and setting up bird feeders and bug hotels. Obviously this will also add to the attractiveness of the garden for humans too!

Installing artificial grass is a big investment, so if you decide to pursue this option, research it thoroughly first, so you make the right choices. Different lengths of grass, colours and densities are available, so shop around, obtaining samples, quotations and if possible, view an installed lawn before committing to purchase. Take into account the practicalities: a really long 'pile' length looks luxuriant but is possibly best avoided because it will make picking up poop more difficult.

You definitely get what you pay for: quality can vary considerably. Enquire about guarantees – some have as long as a twenty year guarantee – but these may depend on whether it is professionally laid or you settle for a DIY job. Installation is expensive, but correct preparation and laying of the surface is key to its success; it is also likely to be done a lot more quickly by professionals who have both the skills and equipment. Once in place, you will only need to wait 24 hours for it to settle before letting your dogs loose on it, making it a very instant lawn solution.

If you aren't sure whether it is for you, or want to find out more, social media is perfect – go online on dog forums and Facebook and ask other dog owners about their personal experiences and recommendations.

7
PLANTS

For most people, plants are an important feature in the garden, providing interest with structure, colour, scent, texture and movement; but if you want to keep your garden looking in reasonably good shape, you may need to select them with your dog in mind as well as yourself.

Right plant, right place

Choose the right plants for the right place; it's one of the first rules of gardening. As well as considering soil and aspect, also take into account your dog, choosing plants which are tough enough to bounce back and not suffer unduly from any accidental damage that might occur. More fragile plants can still be grown – but try settling them in containers, or to the rear of beds where they will have protection from the odd knock.

Young plants and seedlings

Sowing seeds is a much more economical option than buying young plants from nurseries; however seedlings are unlikely to survive a trampling from your dog's paws, and a newly prepared seed bed can look very inviting to him. Unless you are absolutely confident that your 'keep off' lessons are established, either temporarily fence off nursery beds (this is easy enough to do using wire netting and bamboo canes) or grow them on individually in pots until they are larger and more robust. Plant them out as densely as manageable so that as little soil is visible as possible.

Toxicity

Nibbling is not good for your plants and not necessarily always good for your pet either. Many dog owners have gardens stuffed with plants that are well known for their toxicity, and never have any trouble, but you will need to decide for yourself whether to risk doing the same or not. It is worth bearing in mind though, that young dogs and puppies especially, tend to explore the world by both tasting it and testing it with their teeth.

If you have a dog that likes to feast on blackberries while out on walks in the autumn, be very careful about any plants in the garden which carry toxic berries, in case he adopts the same pick-your-own policy.

Some dogs will put absolutely anything in their mouths, no matter how horrible it may taste, and within the limited space of a garden may be more inclined to experiment unwisely. As well as teaching him that your plants are not on the menu (see *New arrivals* and *Edibles* below), it is therefore important to ensure that you establish good 'leave it' and 'give it' commands just in case you do see him chewing on something that he shouldn't be – for his sake as well as that of the plant.

Not all plants described as 'toxic' or 'poisonous' are fatal: some produce unpleasant but not terminal symptoms. How dangerous it may be to your dog depends on his size, age, weight and health status, and the part of the plant and quantity eaten. You'll find details of a few 'dog friendly' plants, and those which you might deem best avoided in the appendices at the end of this book.

New arrivals

Dogs are generally far more observant and aware of their surroundings and changes to it than humans, so new arrivals in the garden are highly likely to attract his interest. When planting out anything new, keep an eye on him; boys may also try and scent mark on them, and even though you may have a toilet area which he uses, once anointed this can then become a regularly visited place to renew the pee-graffiti to the detriment of the plant's health. Be ready to intervene if he shows too close an interest, (see Chapter 3) and to distract him with food, a game or attention.

Continue to keep an eye on him until you are sure the novelty has worn off!

Sniff this

Scent plays an enormously important role in your dog's life, and is one of the senses that seems to remain pretty good right into old age. With this in mind, you might like to consider creating sensory areas for your dog, so that while you enjoy the colours and variety of flowers and foliage, he can appreciate their aromas. You can also select plants which will have a soporific effect, encouraging calm behaviour when in the garden. Not all plants have a pleasant smell, and you can use these – such as the 'Go-Away' plant (see Chapter 5) – to discourage him from certain areas.

Placing plants with different scents or scent combinations in various key areas will also help elderly dogs whose sight is beginning to fail, enabling them to orient themselves and safely navigate their way around the garden, thereby avoiding accidental damage. Information on creating a sensory garden for your dog can be found in Appendix 3.

Edibles
When it comes to growing fruit and veg, the temptation may be too great for some dogs to resist, and they will happily gorge themselves on whatever they find. It can be unfair to expect him to be able to exercise the same sort of self-control as a human, so this is one of those situations where it is best to plant your produce in an 'out of bounds' area which is securely fenced off – or better still, apply for an allotment. This will also solve the issue of the potential health hazard should he pee or poo near them.

Some dogs love to graze, and just as you might provide a digging pit for dogs that love to dig so as to focus their attention on one designated spot rather than depriving them altogether of the opportunity to do what comes naturally, you could, if you wish, set up a special doggy salad bar area. You might do this by allowing the grass to grow long in some areas – we know someone who mows a crescent moon shape in her lawn, thereby making an interesting feature of it. Alternatively, grow a variety of plants in attractive containers, such as oat grass, cress, wheat and rye grass. You could even include couch grass and cleavers which are often favourites with dogs, if not with gardeners: but at least in a pot you can keep them safely contained. Provided you work at garden-training him (Chapter 3), your dog will soon learn that he is allowed to nibble at plants in a certain area of the garden, but not elsewhere – in much the same way that he learned that it is fine for him to eat out of his own food bowl in the house, but that he is not permitted to help himself to food off the table or your plate.

8
CHANNELLING BEHAVIOURS

'Environmental enrichment' in the garden is something of a current catchphrase – it is simply a fancy way of saying making it a more interesting place for your dog. If you have the space, then as well as including planting aimed at providing sensory stimulation (see Appendix 3) adding a few activity areas will appeal to your dog's sense of fun and curiosity. Creating dog play areas has a practical aspect too, as it enables you to channel some of his less garden-friendly natural urges rather than attempting to prevent them. This will result in a happier, less frustrated dog, a nicer garden, and of course means you can spend less time saying "No!" and "Stop that!"

There is no reason why incorporating play features for your dog into your garden design cannot also be an attractive if rather novel feature for you too – with a little thought, many would also work well in an area which is shared with children.

Do think very carefully about where you site any permanent features as once in place, it may be difficult to change them. Work out a proper plan so you make the best use of the space available; and think through the most ideal positioning and design of such elements so they are easy on your eye as well as giving plenty of scope for your dog to have fun. Don't forget to take into account practical aspects such as mowing beneath or near to it!

You may not, of course, want a permanent feature, so we have also included suggestions for temporary alternatives which work just as well; and being able to add or move items around can sometimes help to keep them interesting for your dog. As well as the design features suggested here, in Chapter 9 you will find further ideas for ways of providing in-garden entertainment which will allow him to satisfy his inner doggy nature without damaging the garden.

Provide a den
Many dogs love denning – so rather than trying to keep them out of shrubberies or digging their own, why not incorporate an outdoor kennel into a space beneath a garden bridge or under a decking veranda? Alternatively, rather than tucking it away and making it a discreet feature, you could make it a focal point in the garden instead: a children's playhouse can be easily adapted, replacing any steps or ladders with non-slip ramps. If you prefer a modest affair more in keeping with a smaller garden there are plenty of attractive traditional-style kennels; or give it a coat of paint – maybe adding spots or stripes - if you fancy making it a little more quirky. If maintenance isn't your thing, and you like a modern look, you could choose a plastic igloo kennel instead. Whatever you select, make sure it is raised slightly off the ground, and that it is stable and won't rock when your dog goes inside.

If you wish, you can make your dog's private place blend into, and become an integral part of the garden by adding a living 'green roof' to it. This can also fulfil a practical function, helping to insulate it and make waterproofing last longer. If the idea appeals, you will find plenty of helpful information online as well as practical 'how to' videos on You Tube. Alternatively, provide your dog with the ultimate green-roofed den by making a living willow igloo, wigwam or tunnel: it is the easiest thing in the world to make although be warned that it will need regular attention as willow can grow very vigorously.

Siting is important if your dog is to use his den: observe him to see which spots in the garden he favours. Before constructing anything permanent and expensive, it can be a good idea to first try one of the non-permanent ideas suggested below.

Non-permanent option: If you don't want to build permanent features such as tunnels or hideouts in your garden, a collapsible fabric or wire crate can be a perfectly acceptable alternative, and is easy to pack away and store. If using a wire crate place a sheet or blanket over the top to give a sense of privacy. Leave the door open so your dog can come and go, using it as he chooses. Another solution is to provide a 'cave' style bed; these are a little like a sleeping bag with a mattress type base which your dog can burrow into. If he doesn't like tunnelling into a bed, then a raised hammock-style, waterproof bed which he can creep beneath may be the answer, and can be moved around very easily so it doesn't ruin the grass.

Make a splash

Ponds can be irresistible for many dogs – so if you fancy a water feature in your garden, you might need to consider what sort will satisfy your requirements while being practical and safe for water-loving canines. Ponds can look great but aren't always ideal – they can become thoroughly stirred up and disturbed by a dog taking a plunge in there. They may also be hazardous if he struggles to get out again because of steep or slippery sides - bear in mind that even a few inches depth of water can become fatal for small puppies and elderly, less mobile dogs.

Rather than trying to keep your dog out, or having to fence it off, it can be easier simply to create a water feature which he can safely interact with if he wants, and which won't get damaged in the process. And if you really have your heart set on keeping ornamental fish, maybe you could settle for an indoor aquarium instead?

It is worth visiting a garden centre that specialises in water features to gain a first-hand idea of the many options which are available. Probably the most popular and easiest to install and maintain is a simple bubble fountain. These are very safe as the water is contained within an enclosed reservoir, but the tumbling water can look striking, provide a pleasantly soothing background sound and be fun for your dog to lick and paw at.

It is a fairly simple affair to set up, whether you make one yourself from scratch or buy a ready-to-fit kit from a garden or water centre. Consult a qualified electrician if it is powered by mains electricity, and ensure that any electrical cables are well concealed and cannot be accessed by a curious dog. If you prefer, you can always opt for a solar powered feature.

Non-permanent option: A paddling pool can provide a lot of entertainment for dogs who adore getting more than just their paws wet. It can be set up during warm weather, is easy to empty, clean and refill as necessary, can be folded and stored when not in use, and you can make it even more fun by floating toys and treats in it for him to retrieve.

Special canvas doggy pools which are self-supporting and don't need inflating are fairly robust, or you could improvise by buying one of the rigid moulded plastic clam shell children's toys, which are also very durable. The base of the latter can be smooth and slippery, so pop a rubber bath mat in before filling, so your dog doesn't lose his footing and injure or scare himself. It goes without saying that you should always supervise your dog when the pool is filled.

Take care where you place it as the lawn around the pool can become a quagmire fairly quickly if he is jumping in and out and getting very excited. If this is the case you may want to put some non-slip matting under the paddling pool too, and maybe to set it up on a patio area if you have one.

Going underground

If you have the space for one, a tunnel can be a fun feature to incorporate into your garden. It creates an extra bit of space for your dog to explore (pop in a bit of 'treasure' from time to time for him to discover – maybe a treat one day, and a favourite toy on another) and to run through, or to enjoy a quiet nap in its shade on a warm day or when he feels like a little privacy.

If it is installed so as to create a raised hump along its length, it can also give him a bit of extra height to stand on, where he can survey his surroundings, while the change of gradients produces a more varied and interesting terrain than a flat landscape.

You may have seen all sorts of ingenious ways of creating tunnel structures in dog-friendly gardens at major garden shows, but the easiest and most practical way for most people is to use a concrete drainage pipe. Excavate a shallow trench in which to lay it, with the entrance and exit graduated so as to lead smoothly into it.

One of the enrichment gardens at Stokenchurch Dog Rescue. The 'den' is an adapted children's playhouse, the tunnel has a decorative entrance and to the rear is a paddling pool. Varied surfaces add interest for dogs and humans.

Choose a slightly higher part of the garden to site it on, or create a little height if necessary - don't be tempted to sink the tunnel low in the ground, or it may be liable to fill with water in wet weather. The remaining part of the pipe above ground level can be covered with soil and then turfed over. If mowing over the gradient is liable to prove difficult, use artificial grass over the top instead. An alternative is to create a tunnel using old car tyres. Dig a trench as for a pipe, stand as many tyres in it as you want so they form a tunnel, and then backfill with the excavated soil to form a flat, firmly packed earth surface to stabilise the tyres and provide a level area inside the tunnel to walk on. Depending on how you feel about it you can either leave the tyres standing proud, as they are, or cover them with artificial grass.

Non-permanent option: An agility tunnel can make a perfectly acceptable non-permanent substitute which you can move around. The tubular type of tunnel can be easily folded away and won't take up a lot of storage space; if you have plenty of storage room, a 'collapsible' tunnel can also be fun: one end is a rigid tunnel, which leads into a fabric tunnel which your dog can push his way through.

If pennies are tight it is worth keeping an eye out at local supermarkets, chain stores and online retailers for items such as tunnels like this one, children's tents, ball pools and play sets; often you can snap up a bargain or two, although bear in mind that they may not be robust enough to stand up to rough usage, so you should supervise your dog playing with them.

Dig this!

If you have a dog who loves to dig – a recreation not exclusively reserved for terriers – then creating a digging pit where he can indulge in this activity to his heart's content will keep you both happy.

Creating a special digging area for your dog is very easy: at its simplest, it may merely be a case of resigning yourself to allowing him to continue carrying out his excavating activities in a place where he has already started. Fill in the hole each day so he has to start afresh each time he visits it and is less likely to move on to new spots. If you have a small garden, this can be unsightly, and making a dedicated digging pit for him may be a more acceptable solution, enabling you to make a tidier, even attractive feature out of it.

Timber is usually the most aesthetically pleasing material with which to create retaining walls, as well as being the easiest to use, requiring only very minimal DIY skills; but if you lack even those, you can always buy raised bed kits which have boards that clip together and can be used to define the permitted digging area.

If your dog has an especial favourite spot, then ideally locate the pit there if possible, as he'll be more inclined to use it. The pit should be big enough to allow your dog room to manoeuvre in: ideally at least twice as long as his body in both length and width. How high you make the retaining walls is up to you; if you have a really enthusiastic digger on your hands, who tends to send soil flying left, right and centre, then increase the height accordingly, remembering to leave a gap for him to get in and out. Raising the height of the walls will also give you more scope for making it an attractive feature, whether by decorating the exterior with stains, paint, a mural, artwork, brush or other textured screening, growing plants against it or training climbers up it.

Slightly loosen the soil within the pit with a garden fork, top up with clean top soil (not bagged fertiliser or compost), and it will be ready for action. Regularly hide toys and treats in there at different depths to keep it exciting and encourage your dog to always return to the same place to dig for 'treasure'. When it isn't in use, cover with a piece of tarpaulin to prevent neighbourhood cats from using it as a toilet area.

Non-permanent option: Many dogs will be satisfied with something as easy to set up as a rigid clam-shell type children's sand play-pit, or a woven mesh rubble sack; however, more serious diggers may become frustrated when they hit the bottom within just a few seconds of work. If your dog is one of these, then you may find that you need to set up a more permanent feature.

9
FUN & GAMES

Playing games in the garden can have a devastating effect on it, but this doesn't mean they are all off the agenda. Simply reserve high-energy games for when you are out on walks, and at home encourage those which are more low-key and will have a lower impact on the garden. This doesn't mean they need be dull and boring – far from it: and by engaging your dog's little grey cells and channelling his natural instincts into a variety of different activities, will provide him with an outlet for those very behaviours that can wreck a garden in short order. Having a whole range of diverting and entertaining games can become particularly important if for some reason your dog cannot go out for his usual walks, and is spending more time than usual in the garden. Here are a few ideas you might like to try:

Food games
- ***Treat dispensing toys***

These toys come in a variety of shapes such as balls, cubes, cylinders and cones, and have hollow centres where treats can be placed. Each requires different techniques and degrees of dexterity to release the treats contained inside.

Different sizes are available to suit your dog; also different materials and textures – some pets may prefer rubber to more rigid plastic. Some can be adjusted to make them easier or more difficult and requiring more persistence to get the treats out; it is even possible to get toys which make a noise as they are being moved around, which can increase their appeal for some dogs. Depending on the type of toy and the enthusiasm of your dog, they can even provide a fairly energetic workout. One thing is certain – while your dog is occupied in rolling, pushing or batting the toy around, he is not actively engaged in digging or chewing or otherwise wreaking havoc on the lawn or your plants! Having said that, you should keep an eye on your dog as he plays, since they may occasionally get accidentally knocked into any flower beds without raised edges, so be ready to retrieve them and replace them in a more open area.

- *Snuffelmat*

This is another handy treat-dispensing game which can be used both outside and indoors. Invented by Dutch dog-lovers, the splendidly named Snuffelmat consists of a rubber mat with holes in it through which fleece strips are threaded. Dry kibble or treats are hidden within the strips and your dog then uses his scenting skills to locate them, and his brain to work out how to get at them.

- *Scatter feeds*

Try scattering kibble or treats around the lawn and then tell your dog to go find it! Dogs love this game – it is the closest he can legally get to hunting his own dinner, and will take both time and energy. If he gets over enthusiastic and starts to scuff at the lawn with his front paws, try scattering over a paved surface instead. A large rubber doormat of the type that has large holes in it to allow moisture to drain through can if necessary be used to contain the treats within a smaller area while still presenting a bit of a challenge in extricating them. If your dog becomes very adept, place a second mat over the top to increase the difficulty.

You can also refine a scatter feed and try Sprinkles™: This concept created by Sally Hopkins uses moist food in grass and aims to get your dog's sense of smell and seeking/hunting instinct working. It is a great stress-buster and can be more tiring than an hour's exercise; it will encourage calmness and can be a good way of keeping him happily occupied when you are busy with garden chores. For more information see the Contact and Resource section.

- *Cardboard fun*

Some of the cheapest and simplest toys can provide the most fun. Fill a large cardboard box with screwed up balls of newspaper and smaller treat-laden cardboard containers such as old egg cartons. Allow your dog to see you dropping a few tasty and strong smelling treats, and some favourite toys inside – and then let the fun begin. If he's a little slow on the uptake, show him how to rummage around to find the titbits, and use your voice to encourage him to seek them out.

Try also saving the cardboard centres from toilet rolls or paper kitchen towels; pop a treat inside, twist the ends tightly and then allow him to rip it to shreds to gain the tasty reward.

Ball games

A fast-travelling or ill-aimed ball can cause damage even without a hound in hot pursuit of it – and when he is, chasing after a ball is likely to result in damage to the lawn, and if you misthrow, can end up with him dashing into flower beds or other out-of-bounds areas to retrieve it: the excitement of the chase can override any training you have established.

You don't need to ban ball games from the garden altogether though; by adapting them a little you can avoid damage to pets or plants, and still allow him to have fun, but without getting wildly over excited. Rather than throwing a ball for example, you might try rolling it along the ground instead so you have more control over speed, direction and distance. Playing piggy in the middle, rolling the ball between two or better still, three or more people so the direction of the ball each time is unpredictable can be more fun than you might think – although do allow your dog to 'catch' the ball from time to time so he doesn't become disheartened.

- *Treibball*

Treibball is another good ball game, and one which you can play together in even quite small spaces. It can be the perfect activity for shepherding breeds, but you don't need a herding dog, or even a madly ball-oriented dog to teach it. All shapes and sizes can have fun, and it can provide youngsters and senior dogs with an activity which presents a challenge without overstressing their bodies.

The idea is that your dog uses his nose or chest to nudge a gym ball forward, and in response to cues from you 'herds' it into a goal. It is a great way of combining mental stimulation with physical exercise, without winding your dog up to fever pitch. It can have additional positive benefits such as developing confidence and self-control, and honing your teamwork and communication skills. There are plenty of step-by-step tutorials and demonstrations you can watch online to help get you started, or plenty of trainers who teach classes

in Treibball.
- *Ball pool*

Not all ball games require the balls to be thrown or rolled – a ball pool can provide a lot of amusement. Set up an inflatable child's swimming pool, a rigid plastic sand pit shell or anything similar to create an enclosure, and fill it with balls. If using a plastic clam shell, place a rubber bath mat in the bottom first to provide a grippy surface for your dog's feet. You can buy big bags of lightweight plastic balls for children's ball pools very cheaply – although they are easily crushed, so if your dog is a chewer or has a large mouth, buy more robust and suitably sized ones. Toss a few tasty strong smelling treats amongst them and let your dog hunt them out.

Brain games

If mental stimulation and challenges are lacking in your dog's daily routine, it can be an underlying cause of destructive behaviour, both in the garden and the house. Brain games may not always be the entire solution, but can often play an important part in remedying the problem.
- *Training*

It is really important to keep up your dog's training throughout the whole of his life – the phrase 'use it or lose it' really does apply. As well as ensuring that your dog will behave as you wish while out in public, keeping training up to scratch will make it easier for you to direct his actions while in the garden. Spending a little time each day doing some training can also be a nice way of interacting with each other, and as your dog grows older, keeping his brain active can be as essential for his wellbeing as when younger.

The garden can be the perfect intermediate place for training new behaviours, before teaching the same ones in more distracting environments. You will also find that one of the spin-off benefits of training is that a short session can be as tiring for your dog as a more active game – but training will be entirely non-damaging, unlike tearing madly around after a toy!

If you (or your dog) tend to view training as being a bit of a boring chore, then you simply haven't yet found the right approach. If you haven't tried it already, give clicker training a go - it can be really good fun for both you and your dog, and is perfect for those who find formal training a bit of a turn off or hard to keep up. It's also a very effective training method which actively encourages your dog to participate in the training process: as well as creating lots of enthusiasm and teaching him to focus on you, he has to really engage his brain and work out what you want, so that what he does learn is more likely to stick. As your communication and observation skills improve you'll find yourselves working as a close team, which can be hugely satisfying and will strengthen the rapport between you.

You can also use games to make training a whole lot more enjoyable, and something that you both will want to do – try the Boomerang Game described below for example.

The Boomerang Game

This can be a great way to begin teaching a recall, or to sharpen it up:

1.

Show your dog a tasty treat in your hand, and then toss it a very short distance away from you.

2.

Encourage him to 'find it!' and once he has, encourage him to return to you, showing him another yummy treat in your hand if necessary, and quickly rewarding him with it when he comes to you, as well as praising him lavishly.

3.
Toss another treat a short distance away and repeat the whole procedure several times. Once he has grasped the idea, and is starting to return to you fairly promptly, you can dispense with giving him a treat each time he returns to you – coming back becomes the reward because when he does so, you throw another treat which he gets to chase after and search out. Start throwing the treat in different directions around you, and at different distances to keep it interesting!

This is just one example of a way in which you can use play and games to make training anything but a chore – use your imagination and engage your dog's sense of fun. There are plenty of books that can help to give you more ideas – see the Further Reading section.

- *Tricks*

You don't need to stop at basic obedience – but if advanced obedience and heelwork isn't your cup of tea or your dog doesn't have the aptitude for it, consider teaching a few tricks instead. Most dogs can master at least a few, and they aren't just about impressing friends, but improving communication skills, interacting with, and giving your dog something else to do in the garden and many have a practical side to them too. Teaching your dog to 'shake hands' for example, can make wiping wet, muddy paws much easier.

- *Puzzle solving games*

All sorts of puzzle-solving toys are available from pet shops and online stores, and aim to get your dog using his brain and improving his eye/paw/nose co-ordination and dexterity. Set up the simplest options at first, and if needed, help him work out how to access the treats concealed inside until he has grasped what is required. Always supervise him, as some dogs may become frustrated or impatient.

Choose sturdily built toys; those made of plastic are easy to clean, but if your dog tends to play rough, it may be best to opt for the wooden versions instead.

Not all puzzle games need be shop bought – you can make your own for next to nothing and your dog will have just as much fun.

Petra's bottle spinning game *(photo: Maddy Casey)*

The internet can be a great resource for ideas: Maddy Casey's simple but ingenious homemade bottle spinner for example, provides endless entertainment for her dog Petra and was inspired by a similar one spotted online.

A few small treats are slipped into the bottles,

and each then has to be tipped to the right angle, at the right speed, before they drop out.

- ***The Muffin Game***

This is another easily homemade puzzle toy which will withstand quite a lot! Simply place a treat in the bottom of each of the depressions of a metal muffin baking tray and then pop a tennis ball on top of it – they are the perfect fit. Let your dog watch as you prepare it, and then encourage him to remove each ball to get to the treat beneath.

Activity games

Although described as 'activity' games, this doesn't mean that they are full-on, adrenalin-boosting activities! Games can involve activity without needing to tear up the turf, and if they also combine a bit of brainwork at the same time, will result in a contented dog who will be more than happy to take a snooze later on rather than prowling around looking for new ways to amuse himself. Try the following:

- ***Tuggy games***

You can buy all sorts of tuggy toys, or very easily make your own by cutting an old towel into strips; plait them tightly together and knot both ends securely. Most dogs adore tuggy games, and even if your garden is tiny, it is the sort of activity which really doesn't take up much room.

It will also provide an outlet for energy other than racing around; but do observe a few rules. Don't get over rough or lift the tuggy toy up high – and certainly not so as to lift your dog off the ground – as it can cause damage to his neck. It is safest to keep the toy low so your dog's neck is at a natural angle. If you have a very small dog this may mean getting down to their level to play. Don't drag your dog along while he hangs onto the toy either, for the same reason, not just to prevent your lawn from being scuffed up by his paws. Tuggy games can be just as much fun if they are gentle ones!

Do teach a good 'give it' command so you can finish each game when you want – this will also be good practice in case your dog picks up anything in the garden which he shouldn't, such as a tool or plant (see Chapter 3). Always finish games at the first sign of your dog becoming over-excited; the idea is to have fun interacting with him, not to wind him up to the point where he is so keyed-up that he will let off steam by resorting to destructive behaviours in the garden, whether a manic gallop around or digging up or chewing on plants.

- *Towel game*

This is a very simple 'find-it' game, but which can provide a lot of fun and encourage your dog to use his brain, nose, teeth and paws to find a treat or favourite toy which is concealed underneath a towel. Start with a small, light tea-towel, and as your dog becomes more dextrous use progressively larger and heavier bath towels, or a blanket. You can also wrap the treat or toy inside the towel.

- *Make a treasure trail*

Gardens can be great places to create treasure trails for your dog, and will allow him to use his scenting, observational and hunting skills whilst still leaving your garden intact. Leave him indoors while you get busy hiding a few treats or a portion of his dinner underneath special 'treat stations'. Upturned plastic plant pots are ideal for this purpose as the holes in the bottom will allow him to sniff out the food, and whatever his size, they will be light enough for him to easily turn over to get to the treat. Choose foodstuffs which are fairly strong smelling to encourage him to use his nose as well as his eyes to hunt out each of the caches. Once all the 'treasure' has been hidden, let your dog out and encourage him to 'find it' using an excited tone of voice. He might initially be a bit baffled, and you may need to help guide him to it and show him how to tip the pot over. After he has discovered and eaten the treat, and you have praised him lavishly for his cleverness, encourage him to look for the next one; it doesn't usually take long for most dogs to cotton on, and before long he will be guiding you to their location.

Once your dog has got the hang of the game, add variety and make the hunt last longer by wrapping some of the treats in a towel, putting others in a cardboard toilet roll centre, or in an activity or puzzle toy as well as having a few quick and easy-access flower pot treat stations to keep him keen. Change the locations of the treat stations each time you set it up so he doesn't simply learn to follow a set pattern, but has to actively search them out; this will keep the game fresh and challenging. Don't place treat stations in any areas which you are training him to keep off, such as flower beds – it is important that you are consistent and don't confuse him by changing the rules about where he is and isn't allowed.

- *Bubble machine*

Catching and bursting soap bubbles is one of those games which is a favourite with dogs and young children alike. You can buy special battery-operated bubble machines which produce a continuous gentle stream of bubbles; alternatively make your own by twisting a piece of wire into a round loop with a handle. Dip the loop into a soap and water mixture and then wave it or blow at it to produce a bubble. If you have a dog which loves to chase balls, this can provide a fun alternative which will be less damaging to your garden as the bubbles don't travel as fast or high as a ball, and certainly won't have an unanticipated bounce. You should, however, check on wind direction first, to ensure that the bubbles don't blow across flower beds or other areas you would prefer you dog didn't trample across in pursuit.

If your dog doesn't show much interest in bubbles, it may be down to that famously sensitive sense of smell – try swopping soapy bubbles for bacon flavour ones which can be bought from pet shops.

- *Hitting the mark*

Set up a 'target' in the garden – a plastic lid from a food storage container is perfect and will stand up to a bit of wear and tear from enthusiastic dogs. Teach your dog first of all to touch it with a paw or his nose - if necessary, place a small treat beneath the lid to encourage him to make contact with it. Each time he does touch it, praise and quickly reward him. When he starts to touch it consistently, start giving a cue word such as 'Touch!' or 'Tap!' each time it happens. Once he associates the cue word with the action move a short distance away from the lid and send him away from you to touch it, returning back to you to get his reward. Gradually increase the distance you are from the target – this can be a good way of using up a lot of energy in a small space and can be a fun way of helping to speed up recalls. Do praise and award a treat each time he returns to you after touching the target.

10
TAKING IT EASY

Not all outdoor activities have to be active! Spending some time in the garden doing some calming activities with your dog will help to create associations with the area as being somewhere to relax and chill out, rather than a place where he feels he constantly has to be on high alert.

Taking a nap
Many dogs enjoy spending time simply having a snooze in the garden, especially if there is a bit of sun to soak up. Your dog will, of course, be more disposed to take a nap if you ensure that he is well-exercised in both body and mind – hopefully you will have found some of the previous suggestions helpful.

You might think that enjoying a nap in the garden is the ultimate non-destructive pastime, but this isn't necessarily the case, and as with playing games you may need to take the initiative. Left to their own devices, some dogs will excavate a hollow in flower beds or the lawn, scooping out the earth to create a warmer or cooler place in which to lie. Others will simply sprawl in whatever place appeals the most to them, circling round and round before flopping down with a contented sigh on top of the comfy nest they have constructed on top of your bedding plants...

The solution is to provide a bed for your dog,

rather than leaving him to create his own. Most dogs will appreciate both the comfort and the insulation it offers particularly if the alternative is a hard, sunbaked lawn or patio – such surfaces can be unforgiving on the elderly joints and thinner skin of senior dogs. If you want to splash out, you can buy special outdoor pet beds and loungers, which can be left out overnight: or a special padded cool mat may be welcome on warmer days. Otherwise, just take your dog's usual indoor bed outside, but remember to bring it in later so it does not become soaked by dew or passing showers. Of course, providing a bed will not guarantee its use, no matter how luxurious, so having placed it where you would like your dog to snooze, encourage him to settle in it by giving him a long-lasting chew or food-stuffed toy such as a Kong (see below). Think too about just where you position the bed – he may be happier about matters if he can keep you in view from his cosy spot. Get to know your dog's preferences; some prefer a bed placed in a shady area, others a sunny spot. Remember to monitor dedicated sunbathers carefully as they can suffer from sunburn and heatstroke.

Kong
There are a whole range of dog toys available these days which can be stuffed with food and treats. Probably the best known of these is the classic conical rubber Kong which also doubles as a throw toy with an exciting eccentric bounce – although we'd recommend not using it in that particular capacity in the garden precisely because of the unpredictability of where it might end up.

These can provide a good alternative to bones; chewing can be a stress-releasing activity which produces a calming effect, so can help your dog to settle quietly. Tightly packed with goodies, they will also keep him happily occupied in teasing out the filling on those occasions when you want to get on with chores such as weeding or digging which you would prefer he didn't try to join in and help you with.

Make sure that whatever toy you buy is sturdy enough and an appropriate size for your dog; where toys are hollow, it is important that they have more than one opening to avoid a vacuum being created which can lead to your dog's tongue becoming trapped in it.

When stuffing a hollow toy, initially pack it fairly loosely with treats so it is easy for your dog to get them out. As he cottons on to the idea you can start to push them in more firmly so he has to work harder and it takes him more time to finish the contents. You can even use a portion of your dog's dinner or breakfast – but otherwise, do remember to factor in the food as a part of his daily ration, or he could end up piling on the pounds. You will find many fun suggestions online for stuffings, including on the Kong website: below we include one which our dogs enjoy on a warm summer day. Because it is frozen, it takes even longer to nibble and lick out every last delicious bit!

Yogurt surprise

Mix a mashed banana and some runny honey with low fat plain or vanilla yogurt, and pour the mixture into a Kong – pack the small hole with a dab of cream cheese or peanut butter first to stop it all leaking out. If you wish, you can make it even more interesting for your dog by adding layers of raspberries, blueberries, chopped up strawberries or pieces of crushed kibble or dog biscuits. Pop it into the freezer; placing the filled Kong into a small, empty, yogurt carton will help keep it upright until it has frozen. If you are in a hurry, simply fill with a low fat fruit yogurt and freeze as before: or if your dog is on a diet or cannot tolerate any lactose, fill with a cooled meaty broth instead. As this can be a bit of a messy treat, the garden is the best place for your dog to enjoy it!

Tellington TTouch® Training
In the summer months, devoting some time to giving your dog a nice TTouch (pronounced Tee-Touch) body work session can be calming and soothing for both of you; it can be as enjoyable and relaxing for you to give as for your dog to receive, so can be the perfect way of enjoying each other's company. As well as helping to change your dog's perception of the garden, it is also a great activity to do with older dogs who may not be as mobile as they once were.

Anyone can learn to do the TTouch body work; no special knowledge of anatomy is needed, and most dogs love it. There are many different 'TTouches', the name used for the specialised ways of moving the skin around. We have included a few simple TTouch body work exercises here for you to try; if you and your dog enjoy them and you would like to learn more, we recommend that you buy a copy of *Getting in TTouch with your Dog* by the method's founder, Linda Tellington Jones. You might also like to attend workshops or demonstrations, work one-to-one with a TTouch practitioner, or watch the TTouches being demonstrated online by visiting You Tube and searching for Tellington TTouch for dogs – you will find plenty of video clips.

Getting started
Be sure to not to lean over your dog while doing the

TTouches, as this might intimidate or frighten him. It is safer for you and more comfortable for your dog if you position yourself to the side of, and just behind his head, so you are both facing in the same direction. This will enable you to see him and to monitor his responses clearly but without staring directly at him which he may find confrontational. It also makes it easy for him to move away if he wishes, without having to go through you in order to do so.

The special TTouches involve gently moving the skin in various ways. They are calming and reassuring, helping your dog to relax, releasing tension and lowering his stress levels. It takes only a short time to learn how to produce a beneficial effect, although the more you practise, the better you will become at it, and the more your dog will look forward to, and enjoy, your special quality-time sessions together.

Spend around twenty minutes on each session, although do not feel you have to keep one eye fixed on the clock; this is just a guideline. Younger dogs may prefer a shorter session, and older dogs may enjoy a slightly longer one, but allow your dog to be your guide in this respect.

Signs that he may need a break include him looking unsettled, moving away from you, becoming distracted, and fidgeting. Stop for a while and allow your dog to reposition himself. If he readily settles down for some more work, continue, but if he responds again in a similar way, then end the session.

Sometimes a dog may appear not to enjoy the TTouches, and if this is the case, stop, but do ask your vet to check him over in case there is a health issue, and then seek the help of a qualified Tellington TTouch Practitioner.

If your dog wishes to move away while you are doing the TTouches, allow him to do so.

Let him choose his position: do not insist that he stands if he feels more comfortable sitting or lying down.

Practise doing each of the TTouches on your own arms or on a partner or friend's arms or back before trying them on your pet. This will help you to appreciate just how light and subtle you can be. Another human can also give you feedback on how it feels and help you to improve.

Concentrating on what you are doing can sometimes make you stiff and tense, which will make the TTouches feel unpleasant to the recipient. Try to relax and keep your breathing deep and regular. Allowing your dog to hear you breathe deeply and *slowly* will also encourage him to match his rate of breathing to yours, aiding calmness and encouraging relaxation.

Just the weight of your hand is enough to move the skin while performing each of the TTouches. At no time should you press into the body; you are only working with the skin.

Make each of your TTouches as slow as possible.

Should your dog show concern about you touching certain parts of his body, return to a place where he is less anxious, and when he relaxes try gradually approaching the difficult area again. Other signs such as stiffness, or tautness or changes in temperature of the skin, or changes in the hair colour, direction and texture of the coat, may indicate the presence of a physical problem; ask your vet to investigate further.

If you are a little unsure about reading your dog's body language and you want to check that he is comfortable with the body work, simply do one or two repetitions of the TTouch you are performing and stop. Take your hands off your dog and move back a little from him. If he re-engages with you by looking in your direction, or moving closer, by nudging your arm or maybe softly whining, then continue doing a few more TTouches. Check in often with him though, by regularly stopping and asking for permission to continue. If your dog moves away when you stop, let him. He may need a drink, or to 'think' about how the work feels. Often he will return and re-engage with you and you can continue but if not, don't force it. Go and do something else instead, play a game, go for a toilet break or finish the session there. Some animals really do need the work drip fed in micro-sessions so be led by your dog and give him the choice.

Llama TTouch
Llama TTouches are very soothing and calming, and can be a good TTouch to start off with, as the way in which you make contact is readily accepted by most dogs

1.
Use the back of your fingers, or the back of your hand. Starting at the shoulder, gently and slowly stroke along your dog's body going with the direction of the coat, and keeping your fingers slightly curved so they are nice and soft, rather than stiff. Do this two or three times, then stop and watch your dog's response – whether he moves

away or leans towards you, seeking more contact.

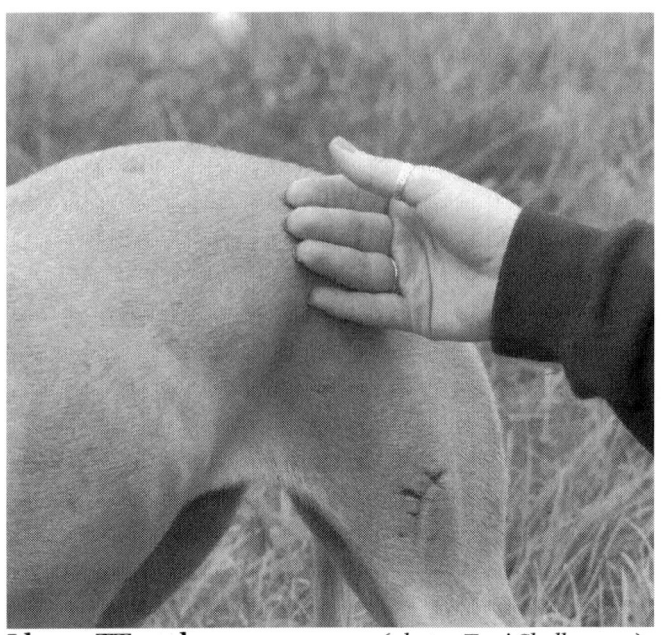

Llama TTouch *(photo: Toni Shelbourne)*

2.
If he is comfortable with the contact, widen the area to include all of him including down the legs and along the jaw line. If your dog appears at all anxious about you touching certain areas, return to a point (such as the shoulder) where he is more comfortable.

3.
As your dog begins to relax, in addition to stroking with the back of your fingers or hand, try making circular movements as well as stroking ones. Very lightly and gently move the skin as you make each circle, rather than sliding over the coat.

Try visualising a clock face on your dog's body beneath your hand or fingers: your aim is to move the skin, going in a clockwise direction, from the point where the six is, all the way around the clock face and back to six again. When you reach six continue without pausing around to the nine so that you have completed one full circle plus a quarter of another one. Pause and then move to another part of the body. Ensure the skin feels as though you are lightly lifting, not dragging it, as you start each circle – experiment on your own arm to check.

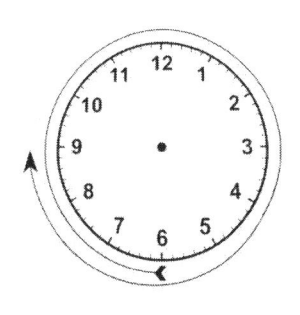

Make each circle as slow as possible, staying soft and light and noting any signs of concern from your dog; if you do spot any, simply stop for a few moments and/or return to a place on his body where he is more accepting of this body work.

Zebra TTouch

This is a good TTouch to use with dogs who are overly sensitive about contact, and may dislike being petted. It's also great for gaining the attention of a nervous and excitable dog, and for calming an anxious one.

1.
Position yourself to one side of your dog – he can be sitting, standing or lying down. Start with your fingers and thumb relaxed and gently curved. Resting the hand on the top of his shoulder, slide it downwards, allowing your thumb and fingers to spread apart as it moves downwards, towards the floor or the feet of your dog.

2.
As your hand comes back up towards the spine, allow the fingers to loosely close together again.

Keep the pressure light, but firm enough that you don't tickle.

Zebra TTouch *(photo: Sarah Fisher)*

3.
Change the angle of your hand slightly each time you complete an upwards or downwards movement so that your hand travels along the length of your dog's body from shoulder to hindquarters in a zigzag pattern.

When you've finished, switch sides and repeat, unless he is lying flat on his side rather than on his chest, in which case just work on the area you can reach.

Ear Work TTouch
Ear Work can have a wonderfully calming, comforting and soothing effect, helping to lower stress levels and heart rate when done slowly. The majority of dogs enjoy Ear Work, and most owners naturally stroke their dog's ears anyway, without even thinking about it!

1.
Position yourself so that both you and your dog are facing in the same direction. Lightly place one hand on his body. Use the back of your other hand to stroke softly along the outside of one ear.

2.
If your dog is happy about this, cup your hand around the ear and stroke from the base to the tip. Try to mould as much of your hand as possible around his ear for maximum contact. If your dog has upright ears work in an upwards direction: if they flop downwards, work in a horizontal outwards and downwards direction.

3.
Next, take the ear between the thumb and curved forefingers of one hand so that you only have one layer of ear flap between fingers and thumb. Slide them along the length of the ear, working from the base right out to the end or tip (*below*).

Ear TTouch *(photo: David & Charles)*

Move your hand slightly each time you begin a new stroke so that you cover every part of the ear. Be gentle and work slowly to help calm and relax. At the tip of the ear is an acupressure 'shock' point: make a small circle there with the tip of your forefinger to stimulate it, and then slide your fingers off. This is beneficial for dogs that are habitually nervous.

4.

If your dog is holding his ears in a furled, pinned or high ear carriage, very gently unfurl them as you slide along each ear, bringing it into a more natural, relaxed position. Posture can directly affect behaviour, so if the ears are relaxed the rest of the body will tend to follow suit.

5.

If your dog doesn't seem to enjoy ear work and has floppy ears, try moulding your hand over one and gently holding it against his head (*below*).

Ear TTouch *(photo: Sarah Fisher)*

Very slowly and gently move your whole hand in a circular movement, so that his head supports his ear. Make the circle small so that it is a subtle movement; he may prefer it being circled in an anti-clockwise direction to a clockwise one. If he still finds this challenging try wearing a sheepskin mitten or glove to diffuse the sensation even further. You may find that this will help to reduce any concerns he has and to become more tolerant about Ear work. If he continues to show concern, do ask your vet to check his ears, mouth and neck, as there may well be an underlying physical reason for his unease.

The Confidence Course
Ground work – also known as a 'Confidence Course' – is a part of Tellington-TTouch Training. It can have all sorts of positive benefits for your dog; what might at first glance look like an obstacle course is actually exactly the opposite, with the aim being (as the name suggests) to promote confidence rather than to intentionally trip up, confuse or impede your dog. Working his way around the courses you set up will make him more aware of how he is moving, and help him to develop better balance, co-ordination and self-control. It is useful in teaching Agility dogs to move more effortlessly and efficiently, and in helping dogs that pull on the leash to find a better equilibrium physically and mentally. For older dogs it can be a great low-impact exercise to maintain flexibility and provide mental stimulation. A further bonus is that it's a great exercise for improving communication between the two of you, and you will often find your powers of observation growing, and noticing the more subtle nuances in his posture, movement and expression. For very active 'busy' dogs who may fence-run or play very boisterously in the garden, paying little attention to you and even less to the devastation they are wreaking on your plants, it can be invaluable in teaching co-operation and focus, and have a calming effect. Balance and body awareness is really important for confident, calm dogs, and the Confidence Course

will promote both.

It is easy to set up a Confidence Course at home; you do not need lots of expensive equipment, but can easily improvise using objects you either already have to hand or can buy very cheaply to provide a variety of different surfaces and textures, and items that produce a slight movement underfoot.

All sorts of everyday items can be used to create a Confidence Course – this should give you a few ideas. Spread them further apart before taking your dog around them! *(photo: Toni Shelbourne)*

Short lengths of plastic guttering, plastic plumbing pipes, foam pipe lagging or old broom handles make great poles which can be laid out on the ground for your dog to walk over. Slightly raise one or both ends of some poles by crushing an empty drink can in the centre to form a rest for the pole; or scatter them in a random 'pick up sticks' style pile which he has to pick his way through.

You might use old bicycle tyres or similar, to create mini-mazes to walk through. A short length of scaffold plank can be stepped over or walked along: raise one or both ends by placing a piece of half-profile plastic guttering beneath to create a low raised walkway. Use pieces of carpet, rubber bath mats, non-slip plastic and other materials to provide different textures and feels beneath his paws as he moves across them – you could even press the doormat from the front door into service! If you have a foam mattress from a garden lounger it will create a surface that yields slightly as he walks across it, giving yet another different experience.

Use plastic squash or water bottles weighted by half filling with water, or empty upturned plastic plant pots, or sports cones to create a slalom for your dog to weave in and out of. Be inventive – as long as the objects you choose are safe, you can create endless variations to keep your dog engaged. If you want to spend a little money and buy some equipment, look online for wobble cushions and physiotherapy equipment for dogs to add to your courses.

You can practice working over a Confidence Course pretty well anywhere you have room for a few obstacles – indoors as well as outside. It is beneficial to vary the locations where you set it up, but start off by introducing it in an area where your dog feels safe and relaxed and there are few distractions: away from the garden fence, for example, or if necessary in the house.

Once you have a few pieces of equipment set up, pop a leash on your dog so you can help to guide him to each one in turn and can encourage him to slow down if he tries to rush. Attaching the leash to the collar can result in an inadvertent tug on his neck raising his head; this can then put him into a state of arousal or unbalance him and is exactly the opposite effect of the one you are trying to create. For preference, use a harness instead: and if it has a securely attached ring at the front of the chest, you can clip one end of a double-ended leash to it, and the other end of the leash to a ring at the top of the shoulders. The two points of contact this provides can allow you to be even more subtle in your communication with your dog – you can find out more about this from the Tellington TTouch online sites and books (see Contacts & Resources and Further Reading).

Ask your dog to approach and slowly move over, through or onto each of the obstacles in turn *(left)* – it is not a race! If he rushes, he is more likely to become unbalanced and to make mistakes. Moving slowly encourages him to move with greater deliberation and precision, developing his physical control and self-restraint.

(photo: Sarah Fisher)

Vary the routes you take around the Confidence Course and the order and direction in which you approach each obstacle. Ask him to stop frequently, both in front of, while standing on, and after completing each piece of equipment, so he can collect himself physically, mentally and emotionally. Halting makes him more aware of his movements, encouraging him to focus his attention on the task in hand and to carefully plan his next move. If you need to give a little signal on the leash to encourage your dog to slow down or stop, remember to do so very gently, and to slowly allow the tension on it to go slack afterwards so you do not interfere with his balance. Remembering to allow this gentle release of tension on the leash is also important in helping to teach your dog to take responsibility for, and re-organise his equilibrium solely on his own initiative.

The ground work may look simple but can be very demanding mentally as well as physically so for both young and older dogs keep the sessions short and make the obstacles easier for them if they are struggling. Keep any obstacles they have to step over or onto low, and any turns they make smooth and wide. This should be a fun exercise for both of you not a route march around objects that are scary or excessively challenging physically.

Once he is focussed on the ground work exercises, you can carefully introduce any perceived threats such as other dogs or people on the other side of the fence, or teach self-control around high arousal situations like cats and squirrels who may enter the garden. With another focus i.e. concentrating on working round the confidence course the 'threat' becomes more tolerable and with the aid of reward based training, your dog can learn to be calmer in the garden, and his ability to listen and take instructions from you while out there will improve. There are many ways to improve your dog's balance and ability to work calmly through the confidence course. If you find that you are struggling, contact a certified practitioner; you can do this via the websites listed in the Contacts and Resource section.

You can see the Confidence Course being demonstrated online. Visit YouTube and search for 'Tellington TTouch for Dogs' and you will find plenty of video clips.

Real Dog Yoga

Unlike Doga, which encourages owners to place their dogs in positions alongside their yoga stances, Real Dog Yoga is a training programme designed to teach dogs postures, actions and expressions which will help them in their daily life. The 30 postures, 15 expressions and 10 actions promote calmness through stimulating the parasympathetic nervous system, and encouraging body awareness, muscle control and communication skills. Created by Jo-Rosie Haffenden (from the popular TV programmes *Rescue Dog to Super Dog* and *Teach My Pet To Do That*), Real Dog Yoga promotes option training, a way for your dog to opt in or out of learning. This is done by using a yoga mat. When on the mat you are training but when your dog steps off it you stop; this gives him the choice to continue, break for a rest or stop altogether. It has been shown that dogs (and humans), take on information much more readily and retain the information if sessions are short and breaks are frequent.

Real Dog Yoga trains dogs using a clicker, (a small training aid which gives a specific sound) or a marker word like YES. This technique tells your dog when he has accomplished the desired behaviour; the click or word tells him if he is getting it right or is heading in the right direction, and the desired action is reinforced with a food reward. A click means food, and he will try to get you to click/feed again by repeating the action he believed earned him the food. In this way you can shape the action, expression or posture you are looking for.

The option contract you make with him however, is that if he steps off the mat, he is taking a break from training and is encouraged to go play, have a cuddle with you or go off for a sniff around the garden, and if he doesn't return to the mat, to call an end to training for that session. At first your dog may need to be taught to take breaks if he is a keen worker, by you taking him off to do other things like play with a toy or have a cuddle, or whatever your dog loves to do best.

Once he is more experienced at the training, and through you being disciplined and stopping the training each time he looks as though he is losing interest, your dog learns that he has a choice. If he leaves the mat, and indicates that he doesn't want to participate in training by returning to it, respect this and stop the session. Often dogs very quickly fly back to the mat but they can be different on different days. Watch out for signs from him that he has had enough. These may include looking elsewhere, sniffing the ground, yawning or licking his nose; listen to him and take a break. Encourage him to drink or play, and take a drink yourself. Like all activities that use our brains, 20 minutes is a good amount of time to spend doing training but some dogs will need less and some will ask for more. If, after a break you invite him back on to the mat and he still displays these signs then it is definitely time to stop. Real Dog Yoga is about working with your dog, not making him work.

As with human yoga, ask for each action, expression or posture to be executed mindfully. This means slowing every action down or holding the posture for longer. When movements are slowed and held, you can stretch the body and help the mind to calm. Dogs taught Real Dog Yoga are often witnessed repeating the actions, postures or expressions, in their everyday life i.e. the act of lying down with his head on his feet or crossing his paws encourages restfulness; or yawning and slow eye blinking communicates to another dog to slow down in their approach or to back off from an interaction. These life skills are perfect for boisterous Labradors or hyper Huskies but any breed of dog, and all life stages, can benefit from the training. Real Dog Yoga can be taught indoors, but is also a perfect activity to teach in the garden, encouraging your dog to be at peace in your precious space and providing an alternative to using it as a race track or digging pit.

Getting started
To get started, you will need:
- A yoga mat
- A clicker
- Lots of treats
- A bowl of water for your dog
- A glass of water for you
- A favourite toy or play area like a ball pool
- Access to a comfy bed
- Two pots: one will be a 'non-active' pot which contains the bulk of your treats and is reserved for later in the session. The other pot will be the 'active' one, used to hold the treats you will count out to work with. Alternatively you can use a treat bag if you prefer. Counting out treats will remind you to take a break and means you don't have to remember how many repetitions have been done of a certain action.

A note on treats - medium or high value treats will mean different things to different dogs. If you are a Labrador, even boring kibble is high value! Have a variety of treats pre-cut into small workable pieces. Try not to use anything that is too messy on your fingers. Sometimes if a treat is too tasty it distracts from the task being taught; however, other dogs might need something really high value to motivate them to try.

It is best if the treats are chewy rather than crunchy so your dog doesn't choke or spend a lot of time crunching it. Also you may use a lot, and for safety reasons, you don't want your dog to eat a large amount of kibble. Tempting treats to use include cocktail sausages, hotdogs, liver cake, small chunks of cooked heart or kidney, healthy, soft chewy small commercial training treats, cooked chicken, ham etc: choose something that you know won't upset your dog's stomach. It is also worth noting that training your dog just after his meal might not be the best option – if he is a little peckish, he will be far more motivated than when he is full and sleepy.

Each dog will differ in the length of time he can concentrate for, but be prepared to take lots of breaks; in fact if he doesn't take them naturally, then encourage him to take a break by having a game with his favourite toy, or taking time for a cuddle - but somewhere else in the garden, not on the mat. The mat is only for when you are working.

If you haven't worked with a clicker before, take time to practise before training so you are comfortable using it; make sure you do this out of earshot of your dog. Timing is everything in clicker training so that you can pinpoint the exact moment your dog performs the desired action. If your timing is not very good, it can result in you clicking an action you don't want, which can end up confusing your dog. Get your eye in and sharpen up your reaction time by practising with a tennis ball; bounce the ball - can you click the precise moment every time it hits the ground?

Even if your dog is used to a clicker, spend some time reintroducing it. If he is sound sensitive either make the click quieter by muffling the sound in your pocket or use a word instead. Click and then immediately feed your dog a small tasty treat. Repeat this until you can see that your dog is anticipating getting a treat each time he hears the click.

Introducing the mat

Once the clicker is his new best friend, lay the mat out on the lawn. He will probably immediately go to investigate it; as soon as he steps on to the mat, click and treat. If he doesn't, throw a treat on it to encourage him to step on or use a treat held in your hand to lure him.

If he remains on the mat you can encourage him to get off again by throwing another treat a small distance away. When he returns, repeat the click and treat when he steps on the mat. Do this until you can see he knows the mat is where all the good stuff happens. If you find he is too distracted in the garden, the process of introducing the mat can first be done indoors.

Try to get him to stand squarely on the mat. To encourage this, stand at one of the short sides and throw the treat directly away from you off the other short end. Your dog will then naturally return straight on and you can reward for four feet on the mat, which is what you want *(left)*.

Once your dog understands that the mat is the place to be, you can start to

(photo: Toni Shelbourne)

introduce a base position. This is either a stand, sit or down. Choose whichever your dog is most comfortable with initially; as you advance you can introduce the others.

Because you want your dog to start to slow down, encourage him to hold the stand, sit or down for three of your own slow breaths.

You may have to work up to this extended period – at first you will have to click and treat after just one breath, building up to two, and finally for three. It may take you a whole session, just to practise that. Observe his breathing; does it start to slow, does his body soften, can he remain focused on you, waiting patiently for the reward?

Once you have reached this point, you will then be ready to start teaching him some posture training.

A few simple postures are included here to start you off; to find out more see Jo-Rosie Haffenden's book *The Real Dog Yoga*.

- **Head turns**

This posture can be taught in the stand, sit or down position and is excellent for stretching out a tight neck or encouraging dogs to look away from another dog on command, so as to encourage good communication skills between your dog and another.

1.
Begin by reintroducing the clicker and the mat, and then settle your dog in the base position of his choice; remember to get him to hold it for three breaths.

2.
Count out 10 treats and place them in your active pot or treat bag, ready for use. Every time your dog makes any movement with his head to the side

(below) click (or use your marker word) and treat. At first you may need to encourage him to do this by luring him with a treat held to the side in your hand; or you might try looking in that direction yourself, or get someone to make a small noise or movement to prompt the action.

It is best to pick a head turn to one side only so as not to confuse him for now. Later on you can teach him to turn his head to the other side.

(photo: Toni Shelbourne)

3.
Shape this behaviour so that each time he moves his head you ask him for a little bit more *(below)*. Repeat until you have done 9 repetitions and then on the 10th, throw the treat off of the mat to give your dog a chance to relax.
4.
Count out 10 more treats and repeat. With each repetition try to give him less help to test if he

(photo: Toni Shelbourne)

understands what the reward is being dispensed for. Eventually you will only treat the furthest turns of his head, and then reward the longest ones.

Note that this will take several sessions, possibly over a few days or even a week, depending on how easily your dog learns.

5.
Once he consistently offers the head turn you can start to name it. As he looks in that direction, say 'Stretch left' (or right, depending on which side you have been working on).

Remember to break often, giving him time to take a drink, (and take a drink yourself), and to do something else. Some dogs need more breaks and/or a longer duration of break, while others need to be encouraged to break.

This posture will not be perfected in a day so keep working at it. Once he has learned it, you can start to introduce the head turn to the other side.

Note: If your dog is elderly, or stiff due to holding tension or from a neck injury, do not do too many repetitions as you could make him sore. Think about how you feel yourself when you return to the gym or an exercise class after a break - you can really feel the after-effects for a few days, and that will be just how he will feel too, so be gentle and considerate. If you are worried about overdoing things, count out the maximum number of treats you want to use for the whole of your training session in to your non-active pot so when they are all gone you know it is time to stop and go have some fun elsewhere in the garden with him.

- *Head on paws (Sad)*

If you would like your dog to chill out in the garden, then teaching him to lie down with his head on his paws can be really beneficial as it can be hugely relaxing.

1.
First of all encourage your dog to hold the 'down' base position for three breaths. Once this has been achieved, count out 10 treats.

2.
Take a treat in your closed hand and hold it on the floor between your dog's front paws. Click and treat every time your dog's nose comes down to your hand/floor to investigate, feeding him from the *other* hand **not** the one on the floor.

3.
After a break, count out 15 treats and again ask for a 'down' encouraging him to be calm by rewarding for mindfulness and concentration on you.

This time do not have a treat in your hand but hold it level with his nose, and then point or bring your pointed finger down to the ground and say 'Sad'. Wait for any movement towards the floor with his head and click and treat.

Shape this so you begin to only reward the bigger movements, until eventually your dog places his head between his paws and rests it on the floor, or on his paws *(overleaf)*. Take a break. You may need to repeat these stages several times if your dog is struggling.

4.
By this stage your dog should know that you expect calmness, and understand about base positions. If he is still getting excited, go back to asking for three breaths of stillness or reduce the value of your treats. Count out 10 treats and when in a 'down', point to the floor and say 'Sad'. Once he consistently does this, start to delay clicking by a fraction of a second at a time so you gradually increase the duration of time he spends lying with

his head on the floor or resting on his paws.

If he breaks the 'sad' don't reward him; just ask for it again. This time ask for a little less so he can achieve what you are asking - you don't want him becoming frustrated or confused. Remember this should be fun for both of you!

(photo: Toni Shelbourne)

Real Dog Yoga really does encourage hyperactive dogs to self-soothe and offer different behaviours, which if he is usually inclined to be a bit manic in your garden could really make a difference. If you enjoyed teaching your dog these two exercises, you can find out more by reading the book or attending a workshop or class – you'll find details in the Contacts and Resources and Further Reading sections.

These are just a few suggestions – there may be other activities aimed at promoting relaxation and calmness which you might like to try, such as doing some massage, or if it is something your dog enjoys, having a grooming session.

Finally ...

Acting on the information and suggestions we have provided, hopefully your precious oasis can also become your dog's playground and an area you can both peaceably share together without conflict.

APPENDIX 1
Dog friendly plants

Until you have got any destructive tendencies your dog exhibits under control, it may be a good idea to stick to pet-friendly plants in the garden. If the lists of harmful plants seem endless, there are still plenty of safer alternatives to choose from. We have suggested a few of our personal favourites here, but you can of course have a lot of fun devising your own planting schemes. Make sure you do your research thoroughly; you will find plenty of lists of both safe and toxic plants on the internet, but always check and then double check the information. The same common names are often given to more than one plant, which can lead to much confusion, so look for the official Latin name when doing your research (and also when purchasing) so you can be absolutely clear as to which plant is being referred to in each case. Having said that, mix-ups can still occur even with the Latin labels – for example, as with geraniums. This has become the popular name for both the largely harmless hardy or common Geranium (also known as cranesbills) and the toxic summer bedding plants Pelargoniums. As you can see, you need to take care when making your selections!

The following plants are all widely regarded as being fairly harmless and unless consumed in large quantities, are unlikely to lead to anything worse than an upset tum if ingested. As a bonus, they are also easy to grow, and if accidentally damaged, won't cost a fortune to replace!

Buddleja - a fast-growing easy-care plant if you have a bald patch in a bed that needs filling;

stunning displays of plume like flowers rich in nectar and pollen attract butterflies, bees and moths hence its nickname of the Butterfly Bush.

Busy Lizzie (*Impatiens sp*) - long lasting bedding plants with masses of colourful flowers which will make a glorious display as ground cover or cascading from pots and hanging baskets.

Californian lilac (*Ceanothus sp*) – these come in different shapes and sizes, carrying thick cloud-like masses of tiny blooms; pink and white varieties are available but we love the intense and varied range of blues best. Bees also adore them and in the summer they will hum with all the activity.

California poppies (*Eschscholzia californica*) - great value for money as they will freely seed themselves and continue to reappear year after year. Opinion is divided as to whether there is any degree of toxicity or not, but in the absence of any definite evidence we've been enjoying the fabulously brilliant displays of colour for years.

Common evening primrose (*Oenothera biennis*) – towering stems producing bowl shaped yellow flowers with a delicious delicate evening scent. Another vigorous self-seeder, so once you've got one, you'll have a supply each year for as long as you want.

Coneflower (*Echinacea purpurea*) – the daisy-like flowers with their distinctive spiky cones in the centre can create a really striking display; there is a lot to love about them and nothing we can think of to dislike! Drought tolerant, they don't need a lot of pampering, will flower over a long period and attract butterflies, while after flowering the seedheads will be popular with birds.

Coral Bells (*Heuchera sanguinea*) – fabulous foliage plants with long, pretty sprays of flowers.

Cornflower (*Centaurea cyanus*) – the star-like flowers of a rich and strikingly brilliant blue are a beautiful adornment to any border.

Forget me not (*Myositis sp*) – lovely pale blue drifts that appear each Spring: a freely self-seeding plant, it's perfect for lazy gardeners especially if you enjoy the spontaneity as they unexpectedly pop up in odd corners of the garden. Tidy gardeners may be less thrilled by this, but they are easy enough to weed out if they grow where you don't want them.

Forsythia (*Forsythia*) – whether grown as a single specimen, part of a hedge or to screen a fence, this will spectacularly light up a dull day in early Spring.

Geranium (*Geranium sp*) – hardy herbaceous plants which form vigorous, dense, sprawling clumps of long lasting colour, these are perfect for helping you to create a cottage garden look with the minimum of effort involved and are suitable for a wide variety of locations.

Take care not to confuse these with the toxic tender Pelargoniums used as bedding or houseplants and which are also frequently referred to as 'geraniums'.

Geum (*Geum sp*) – bright, cheerful, and easy to grow, with flowers produced over a long period: some varieties start to bloom in April and will continue on into late summer or even longer.

Houseleek (*Sempervivum*) – the 'leek' part of the common name is derived from the Anglo Saxon word 'leac' meaning a plant so literally means a 'houseplant'; they used to be a common sight growing on cottage roofs as protection from lightning strike and the evil influence of witches. They can look terrific planted up in a pot or adorning a green roof and will thrive in the poorest of soils.

Lady's mantle (*Alchemilla mollis*) – the clusters of flowers are tiny and low key; this leafy plant really comes into its own when jewel-like drops of rain are caught in the foliage.

Lambs ears (*Stachys byzantina*) – with their traditional associations of gentleness, the soft fuzzy texture of the silvery leaves is irresistible.

Mahonia (*Mahonia sp*) – provides a year round evergreen display of holly-shaped leaves, plus sprays of bright yellow flowers from November to March followed by dark berries which apparently you can use to make wine or rather good jam from, although we haven't yet tried it! They come in a range of sizes from modest to enormous so check you buy the right one for your patch.

Nasturtiums (*Tropaeolum sp*) - wonderfully versatile; they can be used as ground cover, trained to climb up fencing or allowed to trail from hanging baskets – and as long as they have been out of reach of dog fouling, both the leaves and flowers are edible and can be a tasty addition to salads. The seed is easy to collect, so after buying your first packet you'll have a free supply for the following year too.

Poached egg plants (*Limnanthes douglasii*) – another easy to grow self-seeder, which will create a cheerful patch of ground cover.

Scabious (*Scabiosa sp*) – another cottage garden favourite, loved by bees and insects, and which also makes a good cut flower.

Snapdragons (*Antirrhinum sp*) – bought as bedding plants or easily raised from seed yourself, they are available in a wide range of gloriously vibrant colours to choose from.

Sunflower *(Helianthus sp)* – another summer favourite which is hard to resist for its sheer sense of drama – grow dwarf varieties in pots or see how tall you can grow one of the giant varieties: when flowering is finished, leave a few heads and dry the rest to hang up in the garden during the winter for the birds to feast on.

Violas – tough and cheery, available in a multitude of colours, they look terrific in beds, planters, pots and hanging baskets and are guaranteed to give the spirits a lift on the greyest of days; some are even beautifully scented.

Appendix 2
POISONOUS PLANTS

As a general rule, assume that any plant which is harmful to humans is also going to be harmful for your dog. Those which are safe for humans are not necessarily safe for dogs however; ingesting grapes, avocado, onions and leeks for example, can have serious, sometimes fatal, consequences. Even if you feel your dog is unlikely to chew on plants, some can be injurious through contact: another good reason for discouraging doggy excursions through flower beds.

Much of the information available about both harmlessness and toxicity is anecdotal, and is constantly being revised and updated, so always double check when choosing plants for your garden and look for the most recent advice concerning safety. Bear in mind when reading any anecdotal reports that even though a dog may have been observed to eat quantities of a particular plant with no subsequent ill-effects it does not mean that plant can therefore be safely eaten by all dogs. Much depends on the individual's health status, age, size and weight; and in some instances the part of the plant eaten. Ill effects may also occur if non-toxic plants are eaten which have been treated with fertilisers, herbicides or other chemicals.

Many plants described as having 'toxic' properties will do nothing worse than make your pet vomit or cause diarrhoea. Others, however, can be more dangerous, and some are potentially fatal, requiring only a very small amount to be ingested. You may therefore prefer not to give the following any garden space at all:
- Oleander (*Nerium oleander*)

- Yew (*Taxus sp*)
- Pieris (*Pieris japonica*)
- Sweet Pea (*Lathyrus latifolius*)
- Lily of the Valley (*Convallaria majalis*)
- Larkspur (*Delphinium sp*)
- Castor oil plant (*Ricinus communis*)
- Autumn Crocus (*Colchicum autumnale*)
- Daffodil *(Narcissus species)*

This is by no means a complete list of poisonous plants; you can find out more by researching online – suggestions for websites you might find helpful are included in the Contacts and Resources section. Remember that toxic plants in a neighbouring garden can become a potential danger to your dog should they grow under, or overhang fences, so check boundaries regularly.

If the worst happens ...

... and your dog eats something he shouldn't, the onset of any clinical effects can be anywhere between 15 minutes to 48 hours. As soon as you become aware of the problem, don't wait to see if your dog develops any symptoms (which may include salivating, drooling, vomiting, severe diarrhoea, and abdominal tenderness) but contact your vet immediately. Do not attempt to induce vomiting unless he specifically advises you to do so – in some cases it can do more harm than good, and it is usually more important not to waste any time, but to get your dog to the surgery as quickly as possible. Your vet will then be able to administer efficient drugs to make your dog vomit if this is considered appropriate, as well as to provide any supportive treatment. Take along samples of plant (or other) material to ensure correct identification and treatment.

APPENDIX 3
CREATING A SENSORY GARDEN

The concept of a sensory garden has ancient origins, although the notion of making one with features intended to be of particular interest for your dog is a comparatively recent one. The idea is that it will provide interest and amusement: the absence of sufficient mental stimulation of the right sort is often a lacking element in many dogs' lives and can lead to all sorts of behavioural problems.

Many animal rescue centres around the country have embraced the idea of creating sensory gardens for the dogs in their care. Sterile exercise paddocks which have been transformed into surroundings that the dogs can interact with and de-stress in have proved to be very successful in achieving their aim.

Many of them can be viewed online or at open days, and can be a great source of inspiration to help you get started on transforming your own garden into a real haven where your dog can feel safe and relax: do not underestimate just how stressful living in our modern world can be for even the most well-adjusted dog, and destructiveness can often be a symptom of stress.

Incorporating features and textures into your garden which have appeal for your dog as well as being aesthetically attractive to humans can be a refreshingly different but fun gardening challenge. How far you take this idea is entirely up to you, of course; there are no hard and fast rules beyond ensuring that whatever you incorporate into your design is safe.

Otherwise, you can tailor it to suit your budget, your own and your dogs' individual requirements and especial preferences. You might, for example, include a whole range of sensory experiences involving touch – this is the first sense which dogs develop, and remains an important one throughout their lives. Most enjoy being stroked and petted, but will also get tremendous enjoyment from rolling around on grassy areas. Providing a variety of surfaces in the garden will also give different sensations as your dog walks across them; textures might include fine gravel, bark chips, cobbles, smooth and textured pavers, ridged wooden decking panels, and sand. These could be in randomly placed areas, or if you prefer a little more organisation could be incorporated into a patio or garden path, using different shapes and patterns as well as materials to create an eye-catching mosaic effect which you will be able to enjoy too, if for different reasons.

There is, of course, no reason why you cannot combine elements of scent and touch, which can help to make a bland patio or garden path really come to life, turning it into a garden highlight whilst still being a functional feature. Lift a few bricks or pavers, dig out any hardcore beneath and top up with soil to create patches where you can then place ground hugging plants such as thyme which will release an aromatic scent when brushed against or walked over.

These are just a few ideas; you will find plenty more online. But if you do nothing else, do at least consider planting, as this is one of the areas where both your dog's interests and your own can harmoniously combine. While you may admire the form and colour of plants, your dog's interest is more likely to be captured by any movement or noise the foliage makes as it is stirred by breezes - and more importantly still, by their smell. Your vision may be superior to that of your dog, but when it comes to smell, he is streets ahead, possessing around 200 million scent receptors in his nose compared to a paltry 5 million in that of a human, and able to detect subtle nuances that we don't even register.

Choosing aromatic plants which you can both enjoy can be the perfect meeting of minds; and you can also select some with known calming and relaxing properties, such as lavender.

A few plants you might like to include are:

Violets (*Viola odorata*) – sweetly scented flowers which have been popular since Victorian times.

Fennel (*Foeniculum vulgare*) – tall, elegant and graceful frond-like leaves; has a distinctive aniseed scent.

Rosemary (*Rosmarinus officinalis*) – choose from varieties that can grow up to 6ft (1.8m) or smaller dwarf varieties: the evergreen needle-like leaves are strongly aromatic.

Peppermint (*Mentha piperita*) - this distinctively scented herb can be a bit of a garden thug, so is best confined to a pot.

Lemon balm (*Melissa officinalis*) – with a deliciously buttery lemon smell, this can also be invasive so is another plant best grown in a container.

Bergamot (*Monarda didyma*) - growing between 18-36 inches (45-90cm), this is also often called Bee balm because bees love the vivid red flowers.

Lemon thyme (*Thymus x citriodorus*) - there are over 50 different forms of thyme: this one is a low growing evergreen with a lovely lemon scent.

Lavender (*Lavendula spica*) – growing 1-3ft (30-90cm) high, these can be grown as single specimens or to make a lovely fragrant hedge.

Catnip (*Nepeta cataria*) – growing 20-39 inches (50-99cm) high, some dogs are as fascinated by the scent as cats.

Meadowsweet (*Filipendula ulmaria*) – the delicate clusters of flowers have a strong, sweet smell.

Sage (*Salvia officinalis)* – grey-green foliage and pretty blue flowers: earthy, woody fragrance, and a useful addition to the garden as a culinary herb for you.

As a bonus, you might be interested to know that lemon thyme, lavender, lemon balm, basil, catnip, and rosemary are all alleged to help keep mosquitoes at bay – so if you enjoy sitting outside of an evening with your dog it may be worth planting them near your favourite place to relax.

FURTHER READING

100 Ways to Train the Perfect Dog by Sarah Fisher and Marie Miller *(David & Charles)*

100 Ways to Solve Your Dog's Problems by Sarah Fisher and Marie Miller *(David & Charles)*

All Wrapped up for Pets: Improving function, performance and behaviour with Tellington TTouch Body Wraps by Robyn Hood (available from TTEAM offices – see below for contact details)

Bach Flower Remedies for Dogs by Martin J Scott and Gael Mariani *(Findhorn Press)*

Brain Games for Dogs by Claire Arrowsmith *(Interpet publishing)*

Canine Behaviour: A Photo Illustrated Handbook by Barbara Handelman *(First Stone)*

Clicker Training for Dogs by Karen Pryor *(Sunshine Books)*

The Complete Dog Massage Manual – Gentle Dog Care by Julia Robertson *(Hubble & Hattie)*

Dog-friendly Gardening by Karen Bush *(Hubble & Hattie)*

Dog Games: stimulating play to entertain your dog and you by Christiane Blenski *(Hubble & Hattie)*

Emergency First Aid for Dogs – Home and Away by Martin Buksch *(Hubble & Hattie)*

Getting in TTouch with Your Dog: A gentle approach to influencing behaviour, health and performance by Linda Tellington-Jones *(Quiller Publishing)*

Harnessing Your Dog's Perfection by Robyn Hood and Mandy Pretty (available from TTEAM office)

Help Your Dog Heal Itself: Insights into Hidden Problems Through the Aromatic Language of Dogs by Caroline Ingraham *(Ingraham Trading Ltd)*

On Talking Terms With Dogs by Turid Rugaas *(First Stone)*

Real Dog Yoga by Jo-Rosie Haffenden *(The Pet Book Publishing Company)*

RHS Encyclopedia of Gardening by Christopher Brickell *(Dorling Kindersley)*

The Truth about Wolves and Dogs by Toni Shelbourne *(Hubble & Hattie)*

Unlock Your Dog's Potential: How to achieve a calm and happy canine by Sarah Fisher *(David & Charles)*

CONTACTS AND RESOURCES

The references provided in this section are for informational purposes only and do not constitute endorsement of any sources or products. Readers should be aware that the websites listed in this book may change.

CONFIDENCE COURSE EQUIPMENT
Equipment specially designed for dogs:
www.activebalance-vetphysio.co.uk/

EXERCISE
UK listings site for safe enclosed exercise areas:
www.dogwalkingfields.co.uk/

FENCING
Fencing supplies and pergolas: acoustic fencing also available:
Jacksons Fencing
www.jacksonsfencing.co.uk

A variety of effective containment options suitable for use either independently or added to existing fencing:
ProtectaPet Ltd
https://protectapet.com

GARDENING
Keep dogs and veggies separate with an allotment! Help and advice at:
The National Allotment Society
www.nsalg.org.uk

Bunny Guinness' web page is well worth a visit if you feel in need of a little inspiration
www.bunnyguinness.com

Green roofs:
You'll find plenty of helpful 'how to' videos on YouTube, as well as details of how to create an instant green roof at
www.enviromat.co.uk/home
Try also **www.livingroofs.org**
and **www.thegreenroofcentre.co.uk**

GAMES & TOYS
Company of Animals – interactive and treat dispensing toys
www.companyofanimals.co.uk

Kong toys – robust toys
www.kongcompany.com

Nina Ottosson - activity toys and puzzles
www.nina-ottosson.com

The Sprinkles game
www.dog-games.co.uk/sprinkles-tm

Zogoflex - tough dog toys
www.westpaw.com

MISCELLANEOUS
Dog Theft Action
www.dogtheftaction.com

Dirt trapper mats
www.turtlemat.co.uk

Kennels and puppy pens
www.kennelstore.co.uk

Safe4Disinfectant and Odour Killer
www.safe4disinfectant.com

PLANTS
Cat grass
www.suttons.co.uk
www.mr-fothergills.co.uk

The Royal Horticultural Society (RHS) website is a handy resource which will help you to select the most appropriate plants for your garden - and if your local garden centre doesn't stock what you want, you'll also find lists of suppliers.
www.rhs.org.uk

Toxic plants: The ASPCA have a useful area on their website at **www.aspca.or**g devoted to poisonous and pet-friendly plants with accompanying pictures to help you identify them. Dogs Trust also has a handy list you can consult at **www.dogstrust.org.uk**

A 24-hour animal poison control service is available throughout the U.S., Canada, and the Caribbean for pet owners and veterinary professionals who require assistance with treating a potentially poisoned pet: **www.petpoisonhelpline.com.**
In the UK consult:
www.animalpoisonline.co.uk

PET BEHAVIOUR COUNSELLORS
Association of Pet Behaviour Counsellors
www.apbc.org.uk

REAL DOG YOGA
www.therealdogyoga.co.uk

SENSORY GARDENS
If you search online for images of dog sensory gardens you'll find plenty of ideas. Our photo was

taken at Stokenchurch Dog Rescue:
www.stokenchurchdogrescue.org.uk

TELLINGTON TTOUCH
For further information about Tellington TTouch, equipment, books, DVDs and links to online videos or to contact a Tellington TTouch practitioner visit the following TTouch websites. *See also Further Reading.*

TTouch in Australia
www.listeningtowhispers.com

TTouch in Austria
www.tteam.at

Tellington TTouch Canada
5435 Rochdell Road
Vernon, B.C. V1B 3E8
www.tteam-ttouch.ca

TTouch in Germany
www.tteam.de

TTouch in Ireland
www.ttouchtteam-ireland.com

TTouch in Italy
www.tteam.it

TTouch in Japan
www.ttouch.jp

TTouch in Netherlands
www.tteam-ttouch.nl

TTouch in New Zealand
www.listeningtowhispers.com

Tellington TTouch South Africa
www.ttouchsa.co.za
TTouch in Switzerland
www.tellingtonttouch.ch

Tellington TTouch UK
Tilley Farm
Bath BA2 0AB
Tel: 01761 471182
www.ttouchtteam.co.uk

Tellington TTouch USA
1713 State Road 502
Santa Fe, NM 87506
www.ttouch.com

TRAINING
Association of Pet Dog Trainers (UK)
www.apdt.co.uk

Association of Pet Dog Trainers (US)
www.apdt.com

Clicker training
www.clickertraining.com

Really Reliable Recall by Leslie Nelson
(DVD, Healthy Dog Productions)

WORMERIES
Wormeries which will take dog waste can be obtained from:
www.earth-essentials.co.uk/
www.originalorganics.co.uk/
www.wormcity.co.uk/

ABOUT THE AUTHORS

Toni Shelbourne

Born into a family mad about animals it seemed only natural that Toni would be destined for a career with them; she says 'animals just walked into our lives, sometimes arriving injured, others just flying in the window'.

She has worked with dogs and wild canids since the late 1980's; during a long and successful career with the Guide Dogs for the Blind Association she quickly progressed from kennel staff to supervisor and then to staff training. In 1997 she studied under Linda Tellington-Jones and other top Tellington TTouch Instructors, becoming one of the first pupils to qualify as a Companion Animal Practitioner in the UK.

In 2000 she left GDBA to pursue her passion for the Tellington TTouch Method and is now one of the highest qualified practitioners in the UK, working with all animals including dogs, cats, small animals, birds, reptiles, wild life and non-domesticated animals.

In 2001, Toni joined the UK Wolf Conservation Trust, where she went on to become a Senior Wolf Handler and Education Officer for the organisation. Through observing the wolves at close quarters, Toni developed a unique insight into their behaviour which led her to question the prevailing popular ideas about the alpha theory in dogs –

ideas which often came into direct conflict with her own knowledge and observations gained at first-hand.

In addition to her background in animal welfare and conservation issues, Toni edited the UK Wolf Conservation Trust's international magazine *Wolf Print* for two years, has contributed numerous features to national dog magazines, rescue society newsletters and website blogs and made many appearances on TV and radio.

Her first book, *The Truth about Wolves & Dogs*, was published in 2012, and her second, *Among the Wolves: Memoirs of a Wolf Handler,* in 2015. Karen Bush and Toni now co-author the HELP! series, with many more books planned.

In 2015 Toni studied with Jo-Rosie Haffenden to become a Real Dog Yoga Instructor. This learning method was featured on *Rescue Dogs to Super Dogs* and fits perfectly with TTouch.

As well as working privately with clients, Toni runs workshops, seminars, gives talks, webinars and demos with Tellington TTouch and Real Dog Yoga.

Email:
ttouch1@btconnect.com
Website:
www.tonishelbourne.co.uk
Facebook:
The Truth about Wolves & Dogs
Twitter:
@tonishelbourne

Karen Bush

Karen combines working with horses with writing about them and about her other great love, dogs. She has written hundreds of features which have appeared in leading national publications including

Horse & Rider, Your Horse, Pony, Horse & Pony, Horse and *Your Dog*. She is the author of over twenty books including the best-selling *The Dog Expert*. She enjoys gardening and even has an allotment, which are tended under the keen supervision of her two rescue whippets, Archie and Angel.

Websites:
www.karenbush.jimdo.com
www.dogfriendlygardening.jimdo.com
Facebook:
Dog friendly gardening

Contact us at:
Website:
http://tonishelbourneadkarenbush.jimdo.com
Facebook:
Canine books by Toni Shelbourne and Karen Bush

INDEX

artificial grass 35, 52
bark chips 52, 120
barking 28, 29
boredom 11-13
chewing 12, 56, 82
clicker 19, 74, 98
"come" 25-7
compost bins 45
confidence course 93
containers 43-5, 58
crates 16-18, 61
den 17, 60-1
digging 13, 38, 39-41, 65-7
environment 10, 41
escaping 13, 40, 41, 43
exercise 11, 12
fences 40-3
fertilizer
flower beds 27, 37-45
games, activity 77-80
    ball 71-3
      brain 12, 73-7
    food
"give it" 24-5
gravel 38-9, 51-2
"in" 29-30
interaction 9
lawn care 9, 33-4, 47-50
leash 18, 28
"leave it" 22-3
napping 81-2
"off" 27-8

paving 40, 42, 50-1
pee cue 30-2
pee post 35
perimeter 40-2, 49
plants, edible 58
    new 57
    toxic 56, 117-8
    safe 111-15
    scented 120-2
playpen 16, 19
poo 36, 58
positive interrupter 21-2
puppies 12, 16, 56, 62
raised beds 42-3
Real Dog Yoga 97-109
sensory garden 57-8, 119-122
stress 13, 71, 82, 85, 119
surfaces 50-4, 120
Tellington TTouch 84-97
tethering 18-19
toilet area 35-7
toileting 33-6
toys 69, 75-6, 82
tunnels 60, 63-5
training 21-32
"wait" 28-9
walkway 42, 49
water features 61-3
wormery 36

Made in the USA
Columbia, SC
21 February 2018